SINGER
COATS
COTTON
SYLKO
FAST DYE
D.438
BLUE JADE
CLARKS

Introduction

This book is packed with lovely designs that are FUN TO SEW. Fun because the materials suggested are bright and colourful and the embroidery stitches used are attractive and easy to sew. Here you will find lots of things that are fun to own and useful too; there are clothes for you to wear such as the smart Smock Top and things for you to make for your own room. There are lots of marvellous ideas for presents, too.

Expensive materials are not essential; quite the opposite. There is something to be made out of even the smallest scrap of material. If you have any little pieces of felt, embroidery thread and cotton wool, for example, you can make a Roly Poly Noah's Ark of animals, and Mr and Mrs Noah. With cardboard boxes, felt and glue, you can make the Ark as well!

Full-size patterns are outlined for you to trace, and instructions for making the items are illustrated step-by-step, with extra close-up pictures in red squares to show you how to do the essential stitches and methods. (Greaseproof paper is ideal for tracing the patterns, and smaller sheets can be taped together with transparent sticky tape for the larger patterns.)

Not only sewing ideas are included, but some ideas for dyeing as well; you will find a couple of tie-dyeing methods, sure to set you off on other tie-dyeing techniques, together with a delightful shaggy pony stencil that you can dye-paint on to fabric.

I hope that you are going to have great fun making the things in this book and will adapt the patterns given to suit new and exciting designs of your own. That would be best of all!

Janet Barber

First published 1973
Second impression 1974
Published by THE HAMLYN PUBLISHING GROUP LIMITED
London · New York · Sydney · Toronto
Astronaut House, Feltham, Middlesex, England

ISBN 0 600 36103 9
Printed in Spain by Litografia A. Romero, S.A.,
Santa Cruz de Tenerife, Canary Islands, Spain.

My Fun to SEW

Written by Janet Barber
Photography by Philip James
Illustrated by Sue Hertzog-Grant

HAMLYN
London · New York · Sydney · Toronto

Contents

Your Sewing Box

It will help you when you are sewing if you have all the tools and various threads and needles conveniently together in a box or basket.

The sewing box can be a pretty biscuit tin or a wooden box, or a workbox or basket designed for the purpose. In it you will need:

Scissors—large scissors for cutting out material; small pointed scissors for embroidery, snipping thread and cutting buttonholes. Pinking shears which cut serrated edges are used for neatening seams. An unpicking tool for unpicking mistakes.

Needles—in various sizes to suit different thicknesses of material; tapestry needles for cross stitch on canvas; crewel for embroidery; darning needles; a rug needle.

Pins—have plenty! Glass headed pins are pretty and easy to pick up.

Magnet—to pick up dropped pins and needles.

A tape measure; a hem measuring gauge; a ruler—accurate measuring is often needed in sewing.

Tailor's chalk and tailor's chalk pencil—for making removable marks on material.

A soft pencil; dressmaker's carbon—for transferring designs onto material.

A well-fitting thimble—for the middle finger of your sewing hand.

Different kinds of thread—you should have mercerised thread for natural materials; synthetic thread for synthetic materials; cheap thread for tacking; cotton thread for strong stitches; button thread for extra strong stitches.

Embroidery thread—soft or stranded embroidery thread and wool should be kept in a polythene bag.

Buttons—keep these in a small box.

Press studs—of mixed sizes.

Pincushion—draw two circles on felt round a jar. Cut out using pinking shears. Backstitch together except opening for stuffing. Stuff. Sew up gap. Cut a piece of elastic to fit your wrist. Place ends over each other. Hem to pincushion. Wear on wrist while working. Or make without elastic.

Needlebook—cut two pieces of felt $5\frac{1}{2}$in. $\times$ $3\frac{1}{2}$in. Backstitch together down centre.

Hints: *Always keep needles in a sewing book, and pins in a pincushion; carry scissors points down, to avoid accidents. *Keep sewing clean in a polythene bag when not sewing. *Choose thread to match or slightly darker than material

A Sunshine Picture

Here is a cheerful sunshine picture for you to sew, with cut-out felt shapes stitched on to canvas. How to make it is shown below. You could mix the story up differently if you wish—give the lady the dog, turned round, on a thread lead, or make her the flower seller. Or you could put other things into

Any felt left over will come in useful for making other things in the My Fun to Sew Book. Save even the tiniest scraps in a polythene bag, to use later.

MAKING PAPER PATTERNS
1 Place tracing paper over pattern shape. Draw round outline. Trace overlapping shapes separately where required. Cut paper carefully round outline.

2 Place pattern on material close to edges. Pin about every 2in. keeping flat. Push pins through both pattern and material and up again.

3 Cut material roughly round pattern. Cut material carefully close to pattern. Small scissors are easier to use for small pattern shapes.

SUNSHINE PICTURE
1 Trace round edges of felt shapes on picture. Draw round each different coloured shape separately. Draw the man's hidden hand like the one shown here.

your design.

That's the fun of making pictures, large and small; you can use your imagination. And you can use buttons, string, rope, feathers—anything.

You will need: stiff embroidery canvas $16\frac{1}{2}$in. × $7\frac{1}{2}$in.; 9in. squares of yellow, green, red and turquoise felt; suitable size scraps of blue, orange, petunia, mauve and brown felt; skeins of yellow, blue and pink soft embroidery cotton; $1\frac{1}{2}$yd. narrow pink lace; thread; scissors; pins; small and large needle; ruler; tracing paper; felt tip pen.

2 Cut out traced patterns and pin to felt. Cut out felt round pattern shapes, then remove pins and patterns.

3 Using running stitch, sew green bench and blue canopy on yellow barrow, on left side of canvas. Sew grass on right side, then people. Sew flowers on barrow.

4 Sew on barrow wheels, cat, dog, sun (two shapes) using running stitch. Leaves, butterflies, birds, the woman's bag and flowers are sewn on last, with one or two stitches each. Edge the picture with lace sewn on with running stitch.

RUNNING STITCH

Keep needle level and push it in and out of material, making small equal stitches and spaces. To finish off, take needle back to end of last stitch and bring out again.

Patchwork Ball

Sewing geometric shapes of material to each other is called patchwork. This small patchwork felt ball is made out of four octagons—that is, eight-sided patches—and two squares. It can be made out of quite small pieces of left-over felt, and in any colours. Before the last patch is sewn in, it is stuffed.

The large patchwork ball would make a safe, wonderful present for someone very young, who would be sure to love the bright colours.

You can make many other things by sewing patches together—a waistcoat, or a cushion for your room, even a full-sized quilt for your own bed. Ready-made patchwork templates, or patterns, are available in shops. Cut material patches a little larger than the template, so that the raw edges can be turned in.

You will need: small ball 9in. squares navy and mustard felt, or two pieces in each colour felt 2½in. × 2½in. Two 1in. square scraps bright red felt; skein of green soft embroidery thread; stuffing of kapok or cotton wool.
Large ball 9in. squares orange, light blue, dark blue and yellow felt; two skeins pale blue embroidery cotton; stuffing kapok, foam plastic chips, etc; scissors; pins; large needle; tracing paper; felt tip pen; ruler; if possible have a thick plastic knitting needle or wooden spoon handle to help pack in the stuffing firmly.

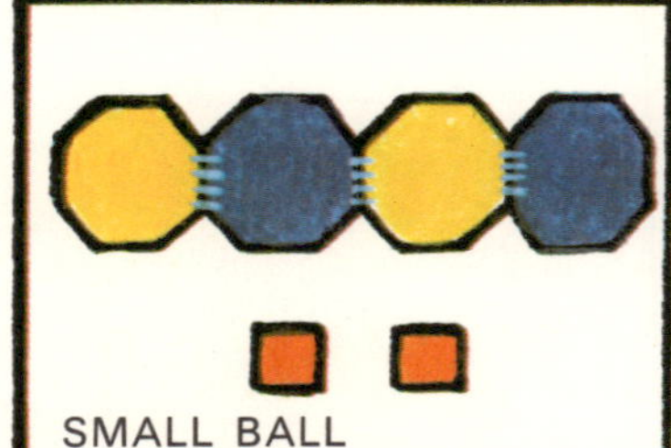

SMALL BALL
1 Trace octagon and square shapes. Cut out paper patterns and pin to felt. Cut two navy and two mustard octagons and two red squares. Oversew octagon sides together as shown.

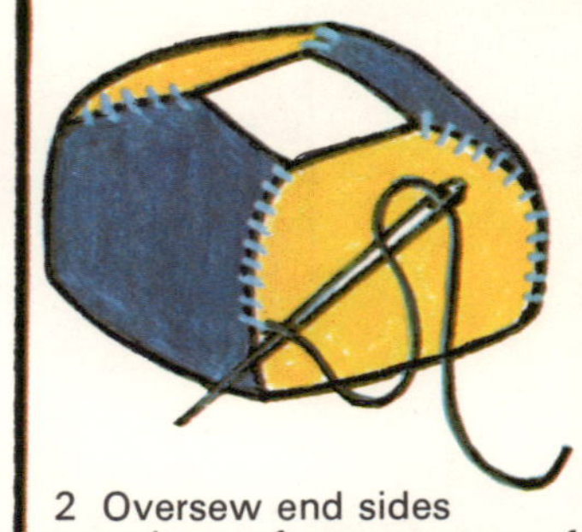

2 Oversew end sides together to form a square of patches. Oversew patches together at angles, top and bottom.

3 Oversew one red felt square into square shaped gap at one end of octagonal patches shape. Avoid stretching felt as you sew.

4 Stuff ball firmly through other square gap, taking care not to stretch felt. Oversew second square shape into ball to close gap.

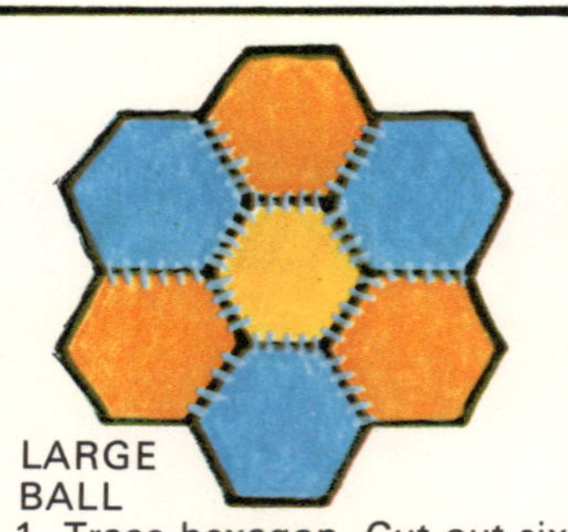

LARGE BALL
1 Trace hexagon. Cut out six orange, three light, and three dark blue, and two yellow. Oversew seven shapes together as shown. Repeat.

2 Trace diamond. Cut out six in yellow felt. Oversew halves of ball together, placing diamonds in gaps. Leave one opening. Stuff. Oversew opening.

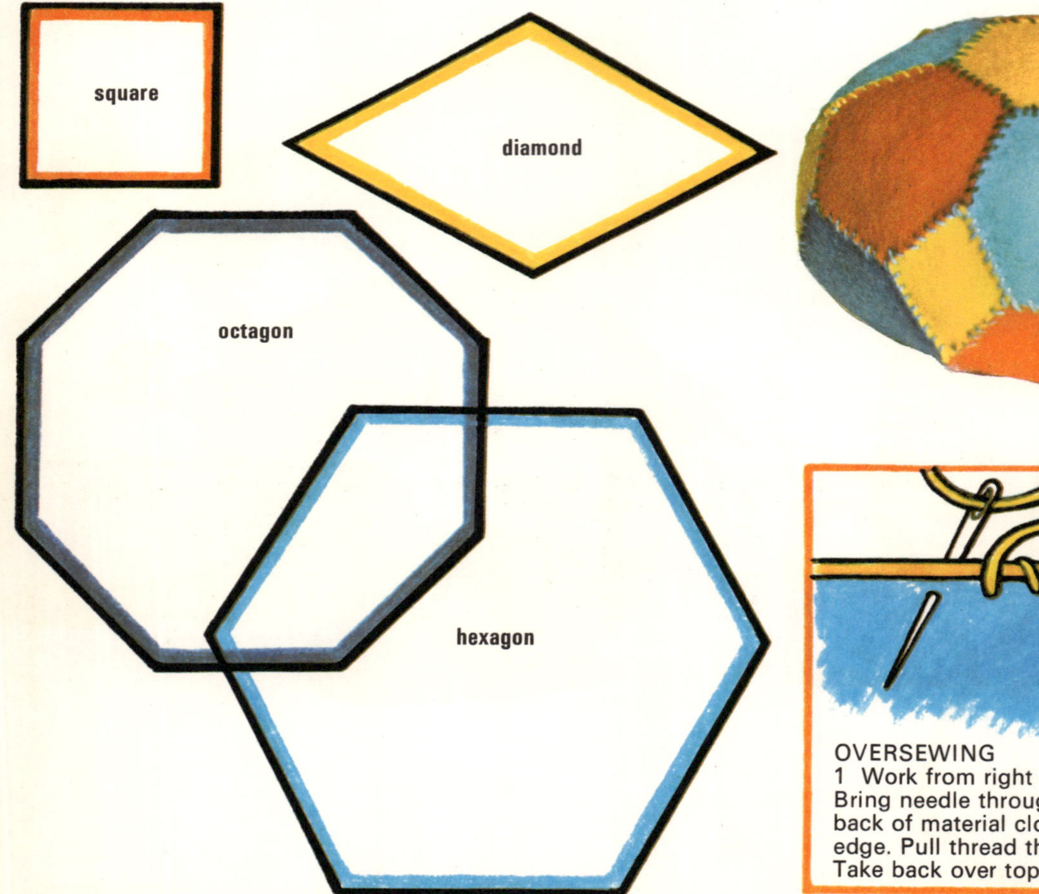

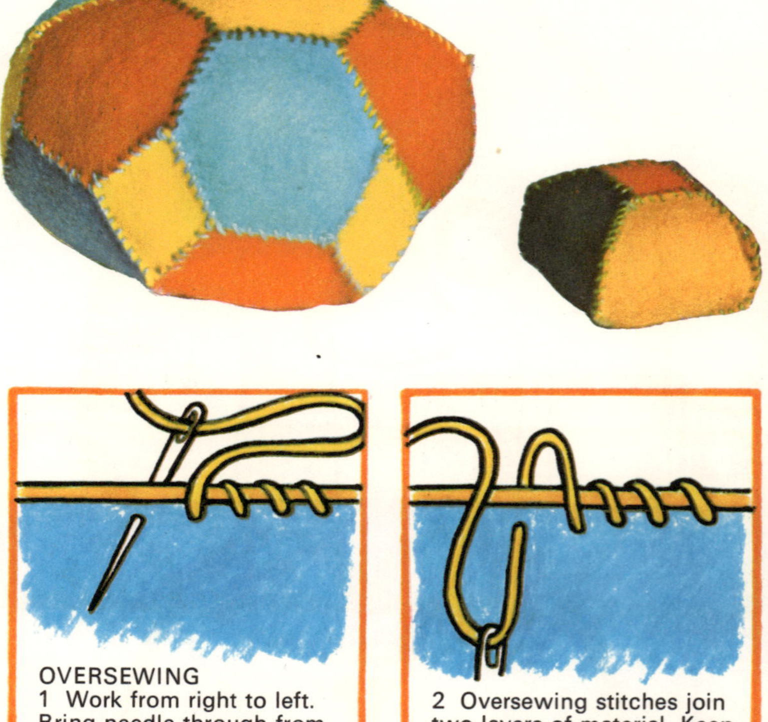

OVERSEWING
1 Work from right to left. Bring needle through from back of material close to edge. Pull thread through. Take back over top. Repeat.

2 Oversewing stitches join two layers of material. Keep stitches the same size, and don't pull too tight or they will pucker.

Mr Trod the Hairy Caveman

Mr Trod is a hairy caveman and the chief of the tribe. He inspires fear and awe in his enemies, and respect from the other hairy folk.

The Great Glyn, seen at a respectful distance behind Mr Trod, is, in spite of his appearance, a useful person in the tribe. He is the peacemaker and also paints the cave walls with pictures when he isn't peacemaking.

Using the patterns on this page, you could make all the hairy caveman tribe, with women too, and children cut out to a smaller size. Some could have long black hair, others bushy yellow hair. Give them seed beads or dress them in leaves (real ones too) as well as fur.

How about making a hairy caveman minstrel or a hairy caveman wizard? Just for fun.

You will need: Mr Trod 9in. square light pink felt or two pieces each 3in. × 4in.; scraps light and dark purple, green and orange felt; fun fur (or plaid) 8in. × 1in.; skeins of green and pink soft embroidery thread; small hank of rust coloured wool for hair and whiskers; stuffing—kapok or cotton wool; card; adhesive; scissors; pins; large needle. *For Mr Trod's friend, the Great Glyn,* pale pink felt 9in. square, or two pieces each 3in. × 4in.; scraps of red, blue, turquoise and bright purple felt; stuffing. Skein of green embroidery wool for hair; pink embroidery thread.

1 Trace pattern shapes for hairy caveman separately, and cut out paper patterns.

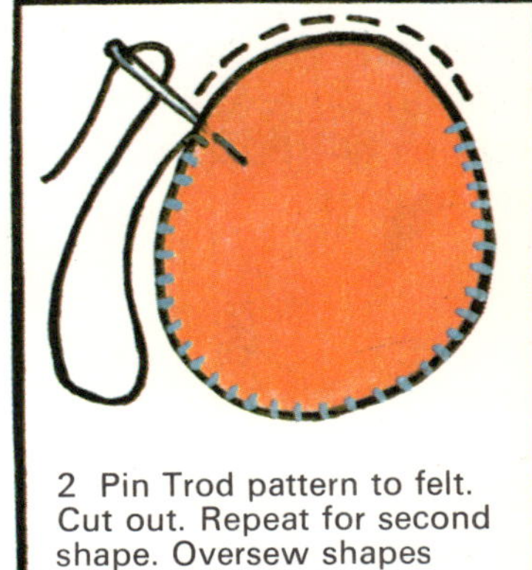

2 Pin Trod pattern to felt. Cut out. Repeat for second shape. Oversew shapes together. Leave top open.

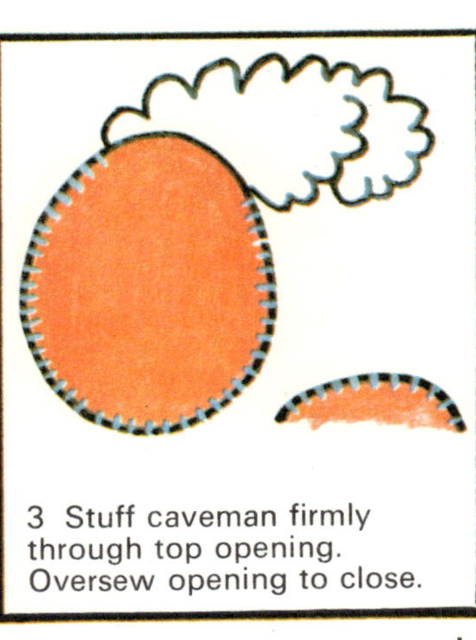

3 Stuff caveman firmly through top opening. Oversew opening to close.

4 Trace patterns for hands and feet. Cut out in felt. Oversew to body. Cut out and glue card feet to felt feet.

5 Trace eyes and nose. Cut out in felt. Glue to face. Cut out fur or felt kilt. Wrap round Mr Trod. Sew.

6 Cut several 6in. lengths wool for hair, and 2in. lengths for whiskers. Sew to head in bunches.

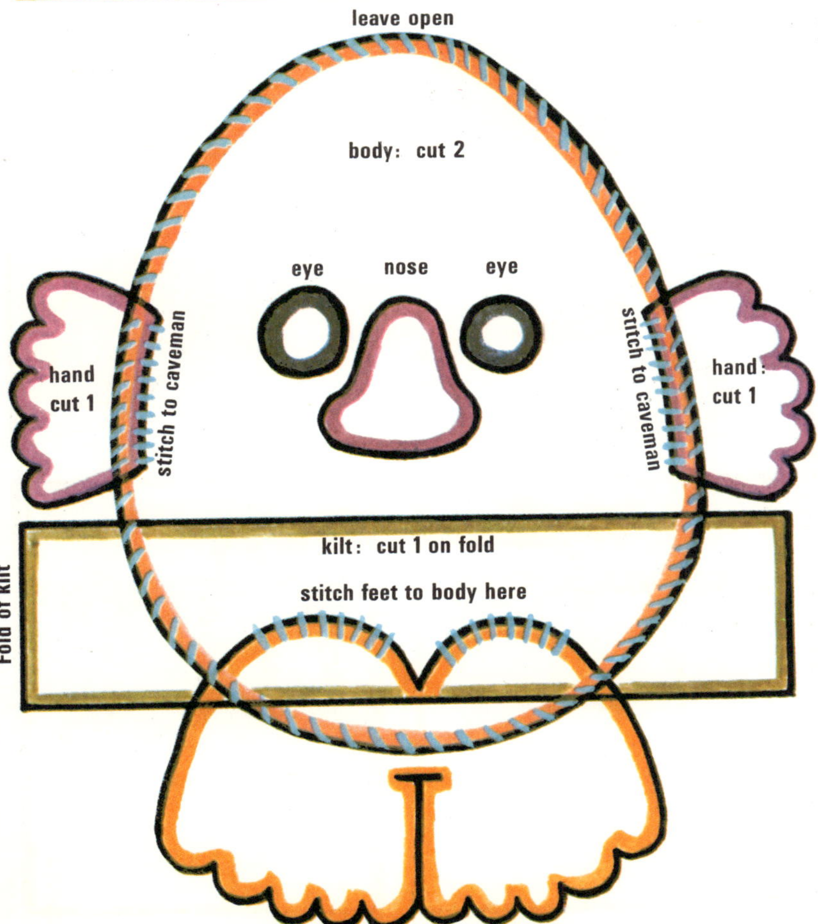

Give Mr Trod a cardboard club glued with felt.
The Great Glyn has 2in. long green hair stitched on at the centre; a mouth, round nose, little eyes and big red ears.

Roly Poly Noah's Ark

Making stuffed animals is fun. And making Noah and his ark and all the animals—two by two—is even more entertaining!

These roly poly animals, as well as Mr and Mrs Noah are all made by simply sewing oval felt shapes together, two or three at a time, and stuffing them. Adapting the same patterns you could add others, giraffes with pencil necks, hippos, cats, ducks, armadillos . . .!

You will need: Mr Noah 2 pieces bright pink felt 2in. × 3in., purple felt $1\frac{1}{2}$in. × $3\frac{1}{4}$in.; red felt nose; black felt eyes; cotton wool beard; *Mrs Noah* 2 pieces pale pink felt 2in. × 3in.; turquoise felt $1\frac{1}{2}$in. × $3\frac{1}{4}$in.; scraps bright pink, blue and orange felt for face and hair; 3in. lace for hat; *Lions* each 3 pieces yellow felt 2in. × 3in.; orange felt strip for mane; *Tigers* each 3 pieces yellow felt 2in. × 3in.; scraps mustard, black felt; *Monkeys* each 2 pieces brown felt 2in. × 3in.; pink felt scraps for face; 2 white pipe-cleaners. *Elephants* each 3 pieces grey felt 2in. × 3in.; red and black felt scraps for trunks, ears and eyes; *Rabbits* each 3 pieces white felt 2in. × 3in.; extra scraps white felt for ears; *Mice* each scraps pale and bright pink felt; *for all roly poly creatures* embroidery thread; stuffing; kapok, cotton wool; scissors; pins; needle; felt tip pen; tracing paper; adhesive.

TO MAKE NOAH'S ARK

You will need: a shoe box and a smaller box. Felt to cover the boxes; card; braid; adhesive; scissors. Glue felt all over shoe box. Glue small box on top, and stick felt around the sides. Cover a larger piece of card with felt and stick on top of small box. Cut out felt windows and door and glue in place. Glue braid under roof and sides of ark. Make a gangway from a card strip covered with felt and a strip of braid.

TWO SIDED ANIMALS
1 Trace animal shape and cut out pattern. Repeat once. Pin Patterns to felt and cut out two shapes.

2 Place two shapes together and oversew round leaving open at top. Push stuffing through opening. Oversew to close gap.

MR NOAH
Make two sided shape. Trace eye, nose. Cut out in felt. Glue to face. Wrap coat strip round Noah and stitch. Glue on cotton wool beard.

MRS NOAH
Make shape like Mr Noah. Cut out face features and hair and glue on to Mrs Noah. Gather lace and sew to head for hat.

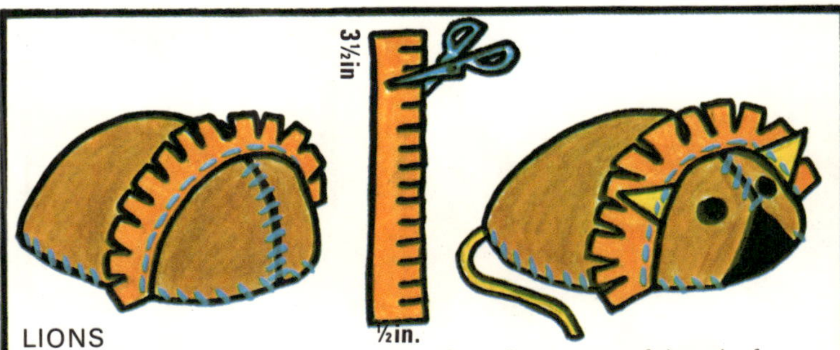

LIONS
Make three sided shape in yellow felt. Cut orange felt strip for the mane. Snip one side of strip to form fringe. Sew mane round lion's head with running stitch. Omit mane for lioness. Trace, cut out and sew on ears. Trace, cut out and glue on eyes and nose. Sew on embroidery cotton tail.

MONKEYS
Make two sided shape in brown felt. Oversew together with pink thread. Sew two pipe-cleaners at centre to back. Bend into arm and leg shapes. Trace and cut out face pattern, and cut out in pink felt. Draw features on face with felt pen. Sew on long embroidery cotton tail.

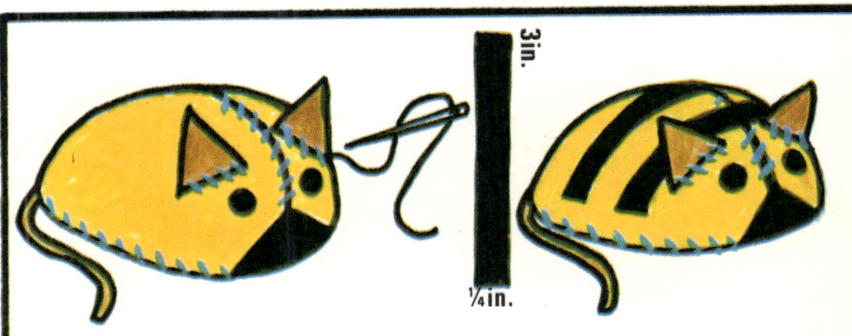

TIGERS
Make three sided shape in yellow felt. Trace and cut out ear, eye and nose patterns. Sew ears on head and glue on nose and eyes. Cut out two black stripes and glue on tiger's back.

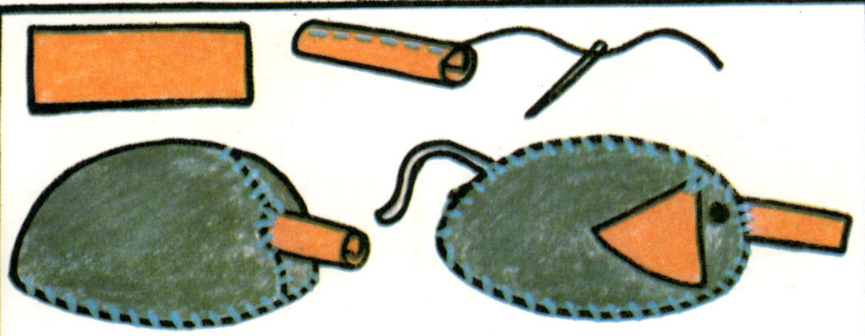

ELEPHANTS
Make three sided shape in grey felt. Cut out a strip of red felt for trunk $1\frac{1}{2}$in. × 1in. Roll felt and stitch down with running stitch; stitch trunk to face. Trace and cut out ear patterns. Sew on ears, eyes and embroidery cotton tail.

RABBIT AND MICE
Rabbit: Make three sided shape in white felt. Trace patterns and cut out two ears. Sew to Rabbit. Stitch black eyes, nose. Glue on cotton wool tail. *Mouse:* trace patterns and cut out three mouse shapes and two mouse ears in pink. Make small three sided shape. Sew on ears, eyes, nose, whiskers, tail.

Leopold the Lion Puppet

Leopold the lion puppet can be made to walk, run or prance by pulling on the strings attached to his feet, head and body. He is strung from two crossed-over pieces of wood.

Other puppets can be made by following the same basic directions for making Leopold. For animals, you would only need to alter a few shapes, the head, colour or material. Or you could invent gonk or cartoon character puppets.

To make people puppets, the body can be about the same size, but two oval shapes oversewn together and stuffed. The two arms hung from the shoulders need to be a little smaller.

To string Leopold, place the two pieces of wood dowelling on top of each other and screw the hook into the middle. Sew strings to the puppet and then tie these round the frame. You can see where to tie each string in the bottom right-hand picture on this page. As you play with Leopold, you will soon find out which strings are too tight and which are too loose. Hang him up and retie and adjust the strings as necessary. Always hang Leopold up by the hook when you are not using him. Then the strings won't all get tangled together.

A stage can be made from a table, with screens and curtains to hide you from the audience as you work the puppets. You can find stories to act everywhere, in books, fairy tales; better still make up your own—especially about Leopold.

You will need: two 12in. squares yellow felt; or $\frac{3}{4}$yd. 36in.-wide felt; scraps white, black, mustard and orange felt; $\frac{1}{2}$yd. narrow elastic; a skein of yellow wool for mane; thread; yellow soft embroidery cotton; stuffing—kapok or foam plastic chips; scissors; small and large needles; pins; tracing paper; felt tip pen. To string puppet: 2 pieces $\frac{1}{4}$in. dowelling, each 9in. long; medium screw hook; fine twine for strings.

1 Trace lion shapes separately and cut out paper patterns. (Draw round a 6in.-diameter bowl for head, or trace from opposite page.)

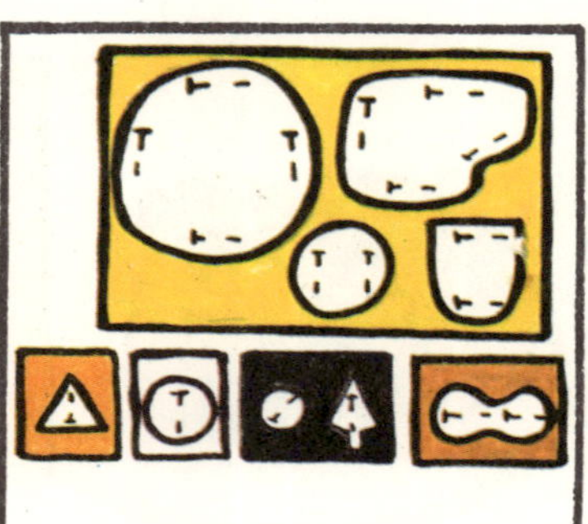

2 Pin paper patterns to felt, and cut out. Repeat until you have cut out the correct number of each shape.

3 Make body and legs. Place shapes together in pairs (one body and eight leg pairs). Join each pair with backstitch leaving openings for stuffing.

4 Turn joined shapes right side out and stuff through openings. Oversew body at tail end to close gap.

5 Cut 2in. piece elastic. Slip into open end of one stuffed leg shape. Pleat leg and sew to elastic. Repeat for three leg shapes.

6 Pleat and oversew open top of another leg shape. Sew elastic to one side. Oversew completed leg to body. Repeat for all legs.

7 Run gathering line round head shape using running stitches. Draw thread tight, to form bag. Knot end of thread, Stuff shape.

8 Slip back of head shape under head gathers and sew together. Fold 4in. piece elastic, and sew to back of head and body front, for neck.

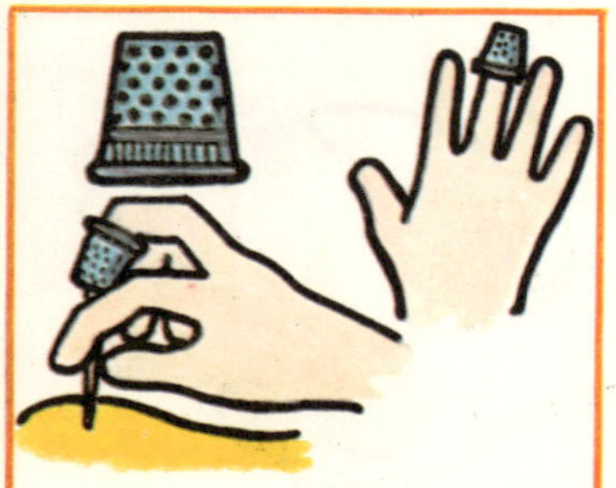

9 Using a Thimble: a thimble should fit snugly over tip of middle finger of sewing hand. Press needle through material with thimble.

10 Sew on mane. Cut 12in. long wool strands. Twist about three wool strands together in a loop, and sew loop to head. Repeat all over head.

11 Trace and cut out face features. Sew whiskers to cheeks. Glue with nose to head. Glue whites of eyes, then black pupils. Make 3in. wool plait and sew on for tail.

12 Sew strings to lion's head, back and legs. Tie to wood. Place dowelling rods together in a cross and screw together with hooks.

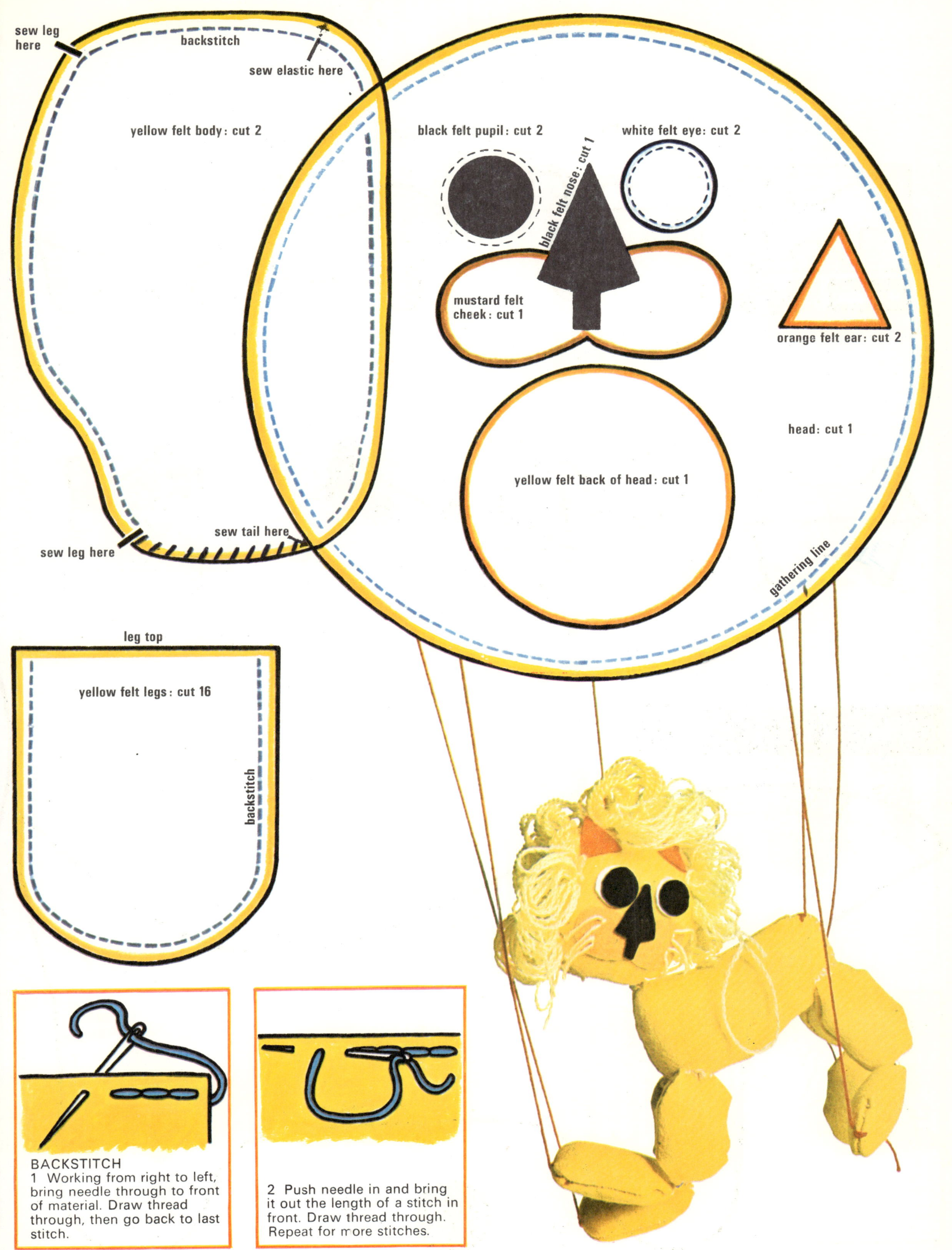

BACKSTITCH
1 Working from right to left, bring needle through to front of material. Draw thread through, then go back to last stitch.

2 Push needle in and bring it out the length of a stitch in front. Draw thread through. Repeat for more stitches.

Patch Dog

Patch Dog may only be a hessian mongrel, patched in various places with rough stitches, but he is someone's favourite as his lost dog-tag shows.

You will need: $\frac{1}{4}$yd. 36in. wide hessian or other material (you could use printed or plain cotton, velvet, needlecord, etc.); scraps black felt for ears, eyes and nose; brown felt scraps for eyes; oddments of brightly coloured material for patches; $9\frac{1}{2} \times \frac{1}{2}$in. strip of P.V.C. material or ribbon for dog collar; $\frac{1}{2}$in. buckle; one small button; thread; soft embroidery cotton; adhesive; stuffing; scissors; pins; needles; tracing paper; felt tip pen; plastic knitting needle.

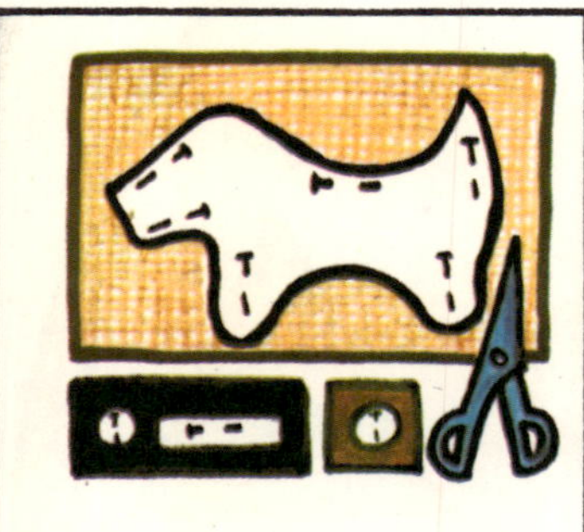

1 Trace and cut out paper patterns and pin to material. Cut out number of shapes as indicated on patterns.

TACKING
2 Tacking stitches are long running stitches, and are used to join pieces of material roughly before sewing properly. They are removed later.

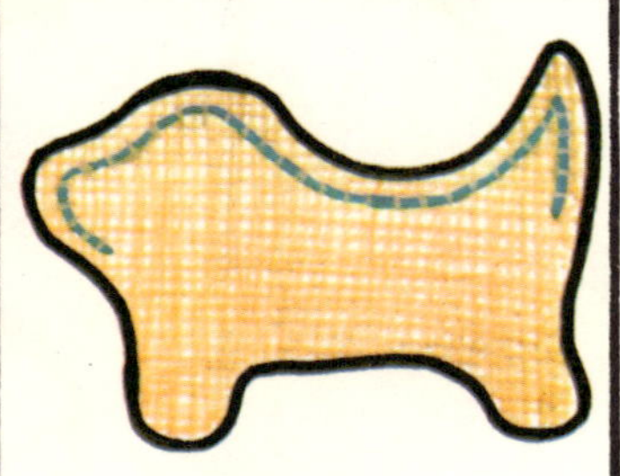

3 Right sides facing, pin and tack sides of dog together along top edge. Remove pins. Backstitch where tacked. Remove tacking.

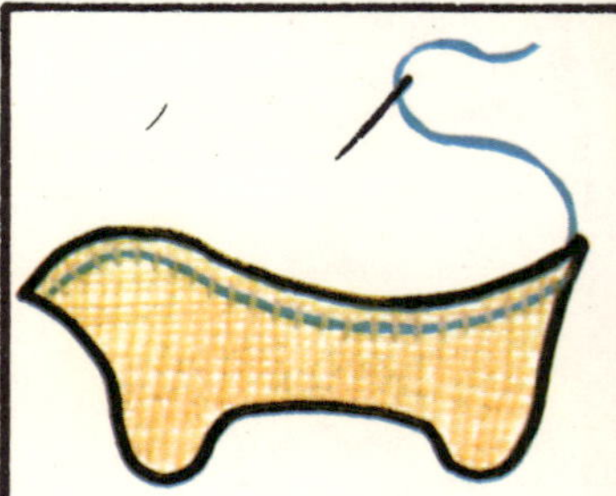

4 Right sides facing, pin and tack undersides of dog together along top edge. Remove pins. Backstitch. Remove tacking.

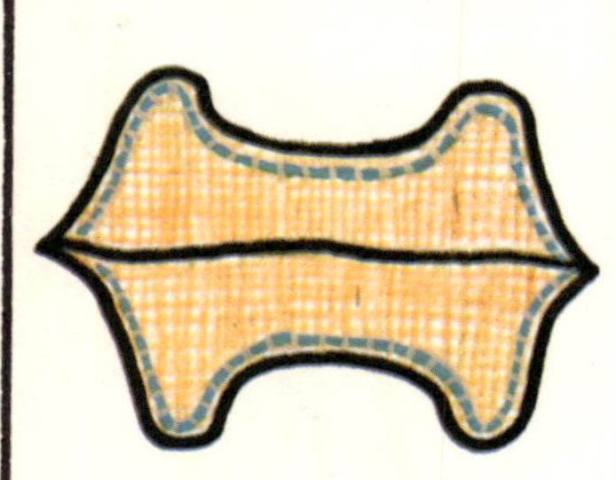

5 Right sides facing, pin and tack undersides to sides. Backstitch together all round leaving opening at tail for stuffing.

6 Turn dog right side out, and stuff through opening. Push stuffing into legs firmly using plastic knitting needle. Oversew gap.

7 Cut out and oversew nose and ears on to dog. Cut out and glue on eyes, first brown felt circles, then black felt circles. Stitch on whiskers if desired.

8 Sew on patches with long untidy stitches. Cut collar strip, slot through buckle and stitch. Sew button on thread for name tag.

When sewing hessian, as this is loosely woven material which frays easily, you must handle it very carefully. Use small backstitches or machine stitches for Patch Dog, with possibly a second row of stitches close beside the first for extra strength.

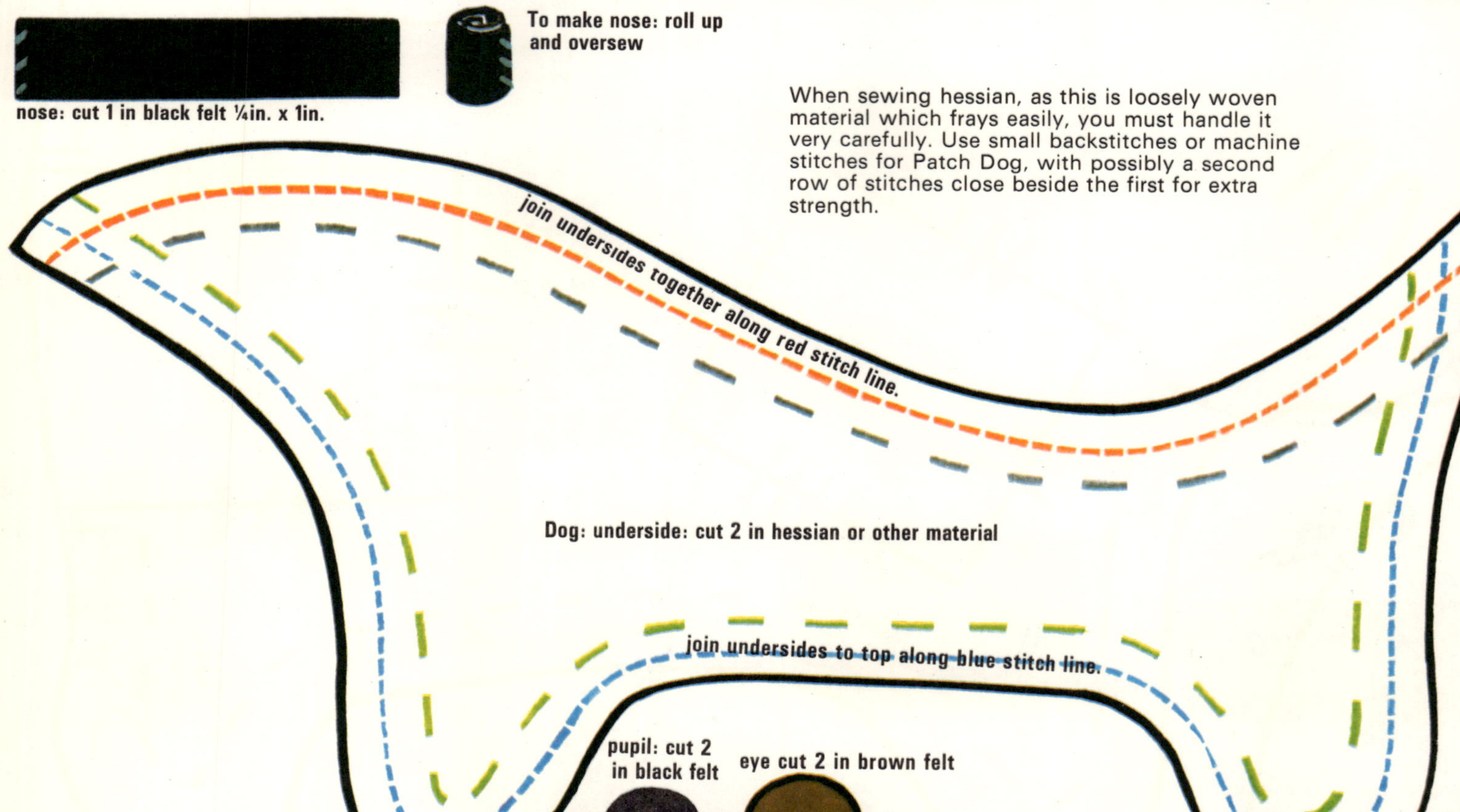

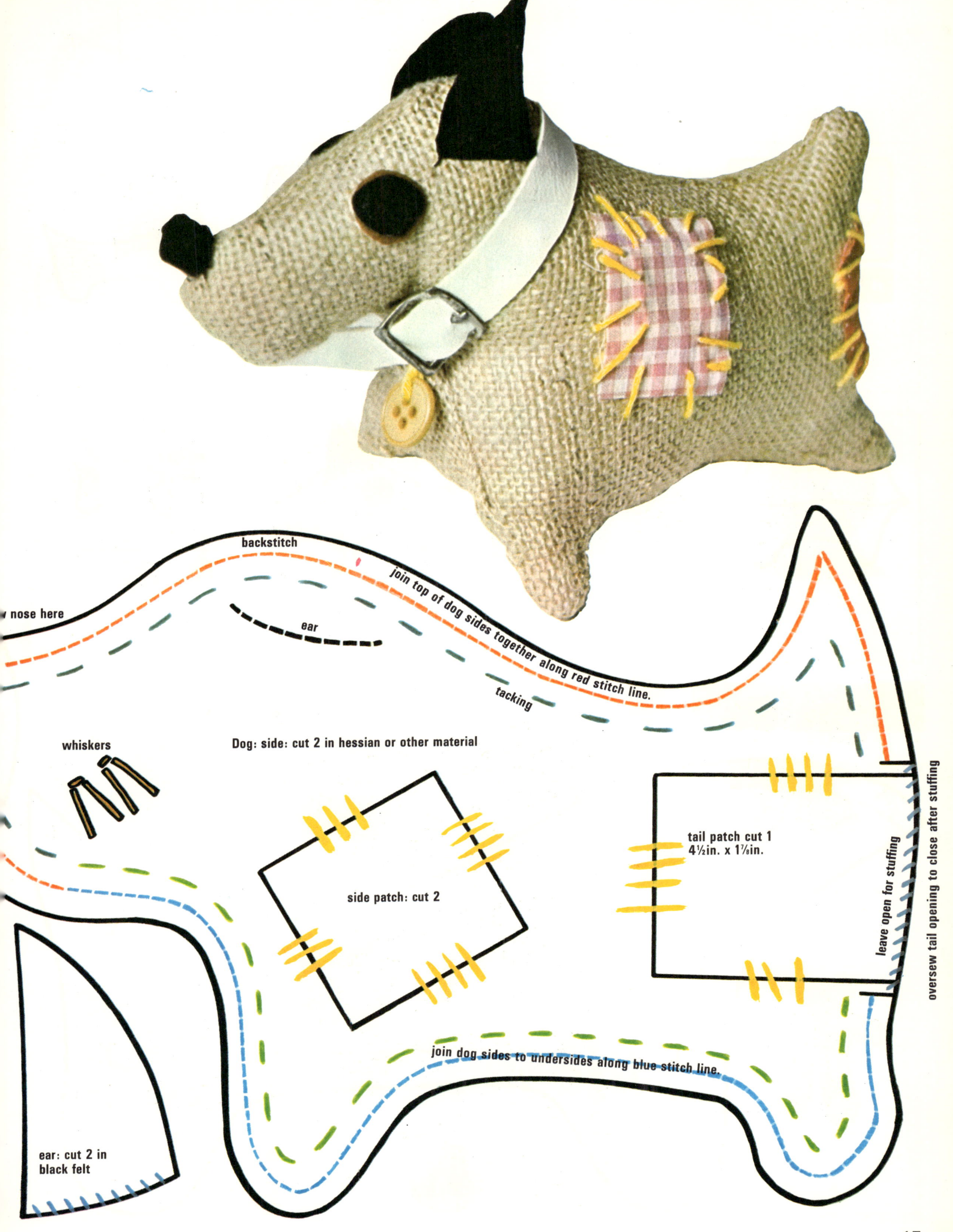
backstitch
nose here
ear
join top of dog sides together along red stitch line.
tacking
whiskers
Dog: side: cut 2 in hessian or other material
tail patch cut 1
4½in. x 1⅞in.
side patch: cut 2
leave open for stuffing
oversew tail opening to close after stuffing
join dog sides to undersides along blue stitch line.
ear: cut 2 in
black felt

Teddy Bear

Of all toys, nearly everyone has owned a beloved Teddy Bear at some time or other. Dressed in tattered pullovers, as time goes by, they end up threadbare, with mended ears and wobbly heads from so much cuddling.

Here is another Teddy Bear to add to your family of toys. He is a traditional kind of Teddy Bear with the right sort of ears and golden brown fur. It is easy to make him because his legs are cut in one with his body, and his face is made by gluing on pieces of felt, with just a couple of stitches for his mouth. He is soft and furry and cuddly, and about 10 to 12 inches tall when complete.

You will need: $\frac{3}{8}$yd. 27in. or wider fun fur (you could use fluffy, soft brushed Courtelle or similar material); 2 pieces pink felt $2\frac{1}{2}$in. × $2\frac{1}{2}$in. for feet; scraps black felt for nose and eyes; thread; black embroidery cotton; stuffing; $\frac{3}{4}$yd. 2in.-wide blue or other colour satin ribbon; scissors; pins; needles, large and small; tracing paper; felt tip pen; adhesive.

*Direction of pile is the way the furry side of material lies. If you stroke it down, it will be smooth; up, and it ruffles. The pile should lie the same way when cut out or it will look different in the light.

1 Trace and cut out paper patterns. Pin patterns to wrong side on fun fur, keeping direction of pile the same, except for ears. Cut out.

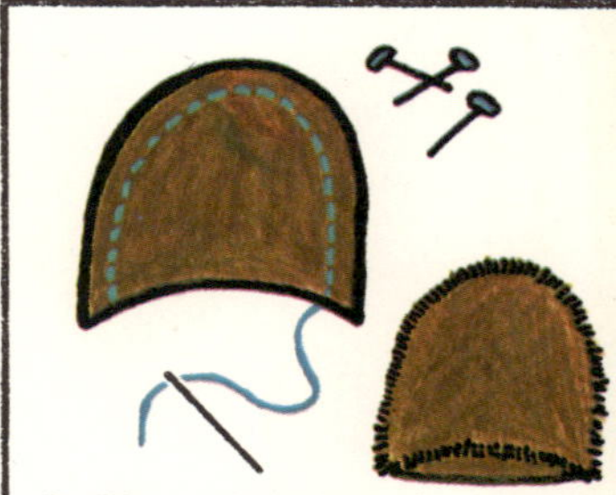

2 Pin and tack each pair of ear shapes together, right sides facing. Remove pins. Backstitch round leaving lower edge open. Turn right side out.

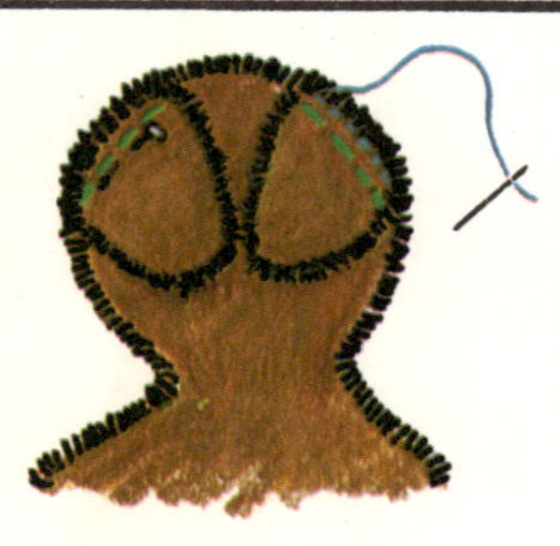

3 Pin ears to front of head, right sides facing, raw edges matching. Tack. Remove pins. Backstitch ears to head. Remove tacking.

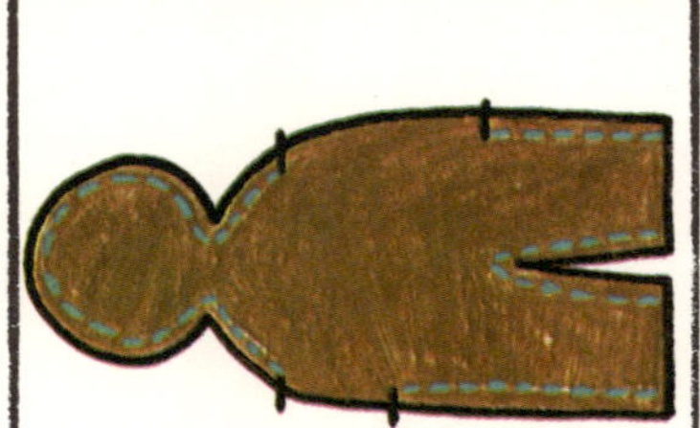

4 Right sides facing, place front and back of bear together. Pin and tack leaving openings for arms and feet. Backstitch where tacked. Remove tacking.

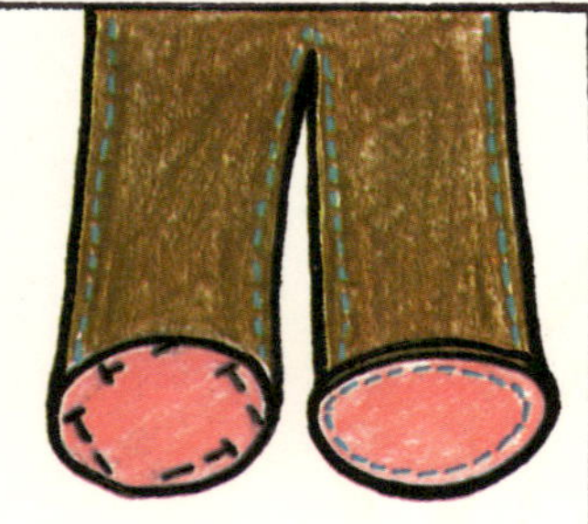

5 Right sides facing, pin and tack feet into ends of legs. Remove pins. Backstitch where tacked. Remove tacking.

6 Right sides facing, pin two arm shapes together. Tack. Remove pins. Backstitch except tops. Turn right side out. Stuff.

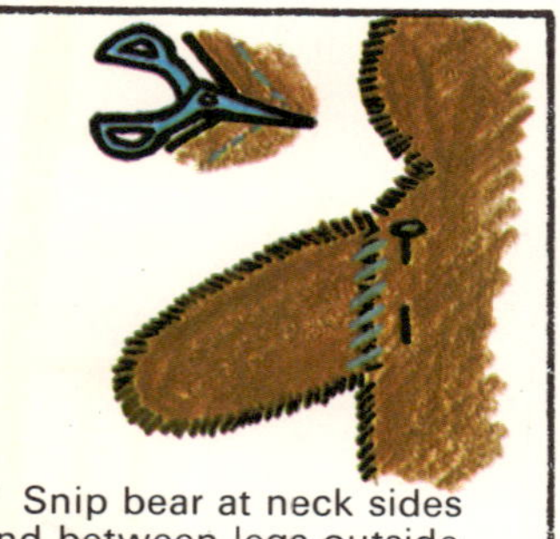

7 Snip bear at neck sides and between legs outside stitches. Turn bear right side out. Pin, tack and oversew one arm in shorter armhole.

8 Firmly stuff bear through long armhole opening. Push in stuffing well into feet, legs, head and body, with a plastic knitting needle.

9 Pin, tack and oversew second arm in position, and at the same time oversew the side opening to close and keep in stuffing.

10 Cut out black felt nose and eyes, and glue on bear. Sew two long backstitches for mouth. Tie ribbon in a bow round neck.

*snip with the scissors outside the stitches so the material will lie flat when turned right side out.

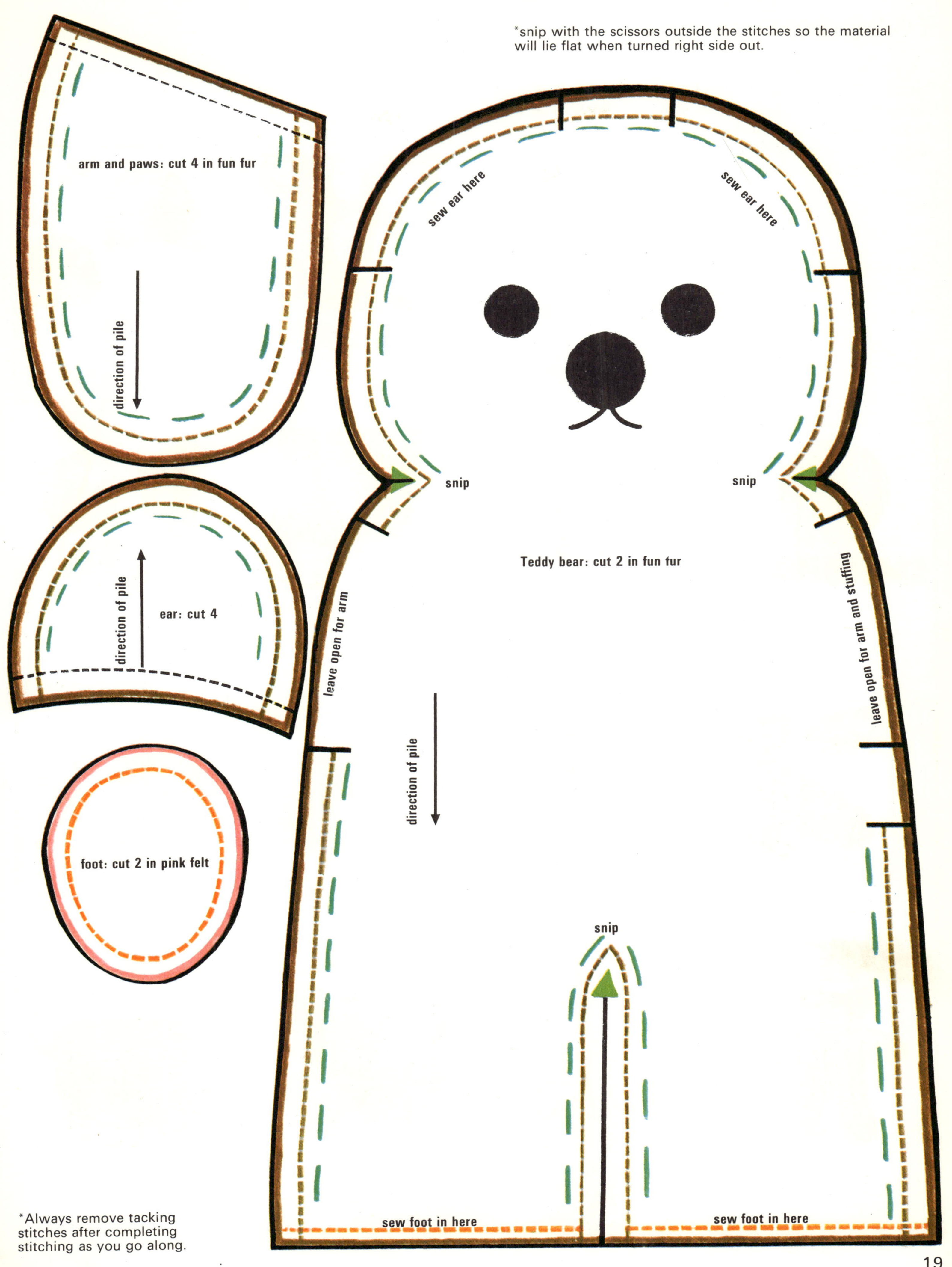

*Always remove tacking stitches after completing stitching as you go along.

Black Eyed Susan—a Teenage Doll

Susan is a teenage doll. She is tall, slim and has thick golden hair which can be arranged in many different styles, with plaits and coils and bows. We have made her the sort of fashionable wardrobe to wear that you may sometimes dream of owning yourself.

Susan's clothes for you to make are on the following pages. There is a cape, with a kilt to match; a long dress which could be used for a nightgown pattern, too, and some other lovely things as well. The full-size patterns for her clothes can be adapted for many other outfits.

How about giving her beach clothes, with a square poncho and a different bikini from the one on this page? She would need a beach bag, and cut-out and painted card sunglasses, too. Susan's fashion possibilities are endless.

You will need: doll $\frac{3}{4}$yd. white cotton sateen (or similar material—calico, poplin, etc.); scraps red, pink and black felt for face; 1oz. skein yellow wool for hair; kapok for stuffing; a large plastic knitting needle to use to push stuffing in; thread; *bikini* 2 strips check gingham for pants and top; pants 10in. × 4in.; top 10in. × $1\frac{1}{2}$in.; $1\frac{1}{4}$yd. $\frac{1}{2}$in. wide red ribbon; scissors; pins; needle; tracing paper; felt tip pen; adhesive.

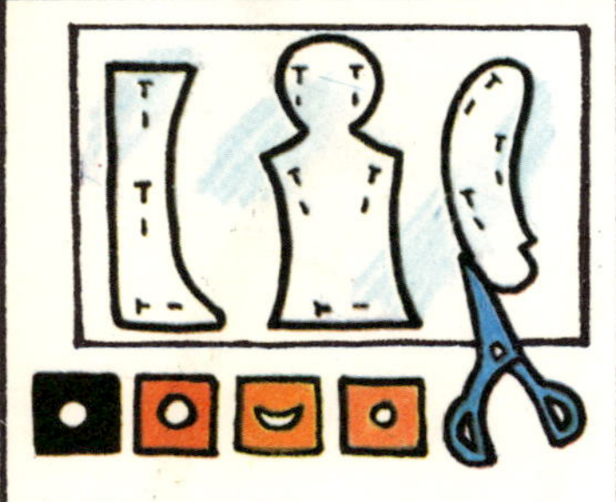

1 Trace and cut out paper patterns. Pin to material and cut out four legs, four arms and two body shapes. Cut out felt face features.

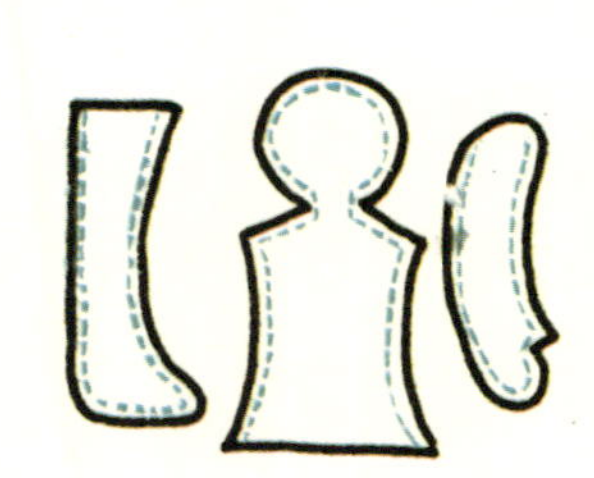

2 Right sides facing, place arm, leg and body shapes together in pairs. Pin, tack and backstitch leaving openings for stuffing.

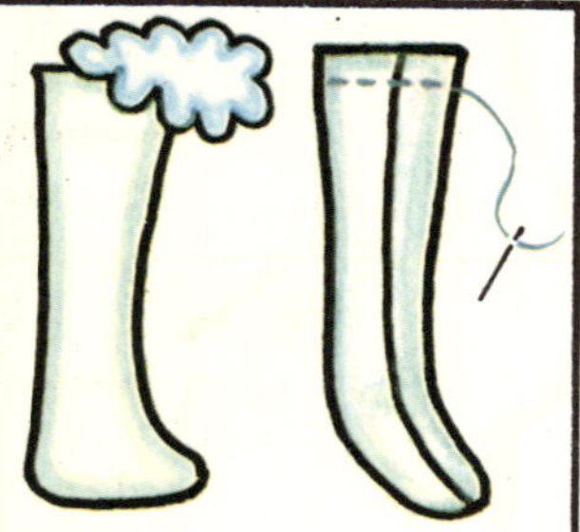

3 Snip legs outside stitches as shown. Turn right side out. Stuff from top. With seams at centre, backstitch tops across stuffing.

4 Snip neck outside stitches. Turn body and head right side out. Turn lower edges under to neaten. Tack. Stuff body and head firmly.

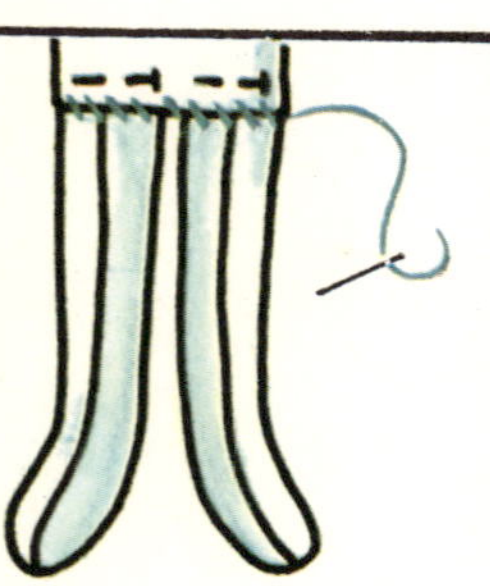

5 Pin legs into body, with leg seams centred. Tack in position. Remove pins. Oversew legs to body, front and back. Remove tacking.

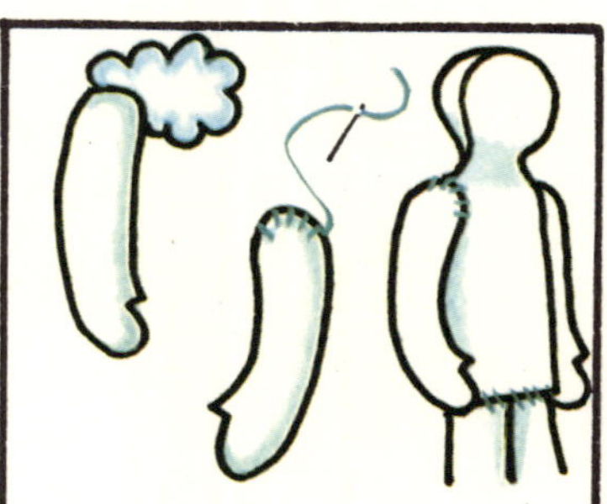

6 Turn arms and hands right side out. Stuff from top. Turn in top edges to neaten and oversew to close. Sew arms to shoulder ends.

7 Hair: sew 12in. lengths of wool at centre, to brow of doll, for plait. Sew 14in. lengths across plait, making parting at centre with backstitch.

8 Plait front half of plait lengths which hang over face at present. Knot end. Fold back and stitch to top and back of hair and head.

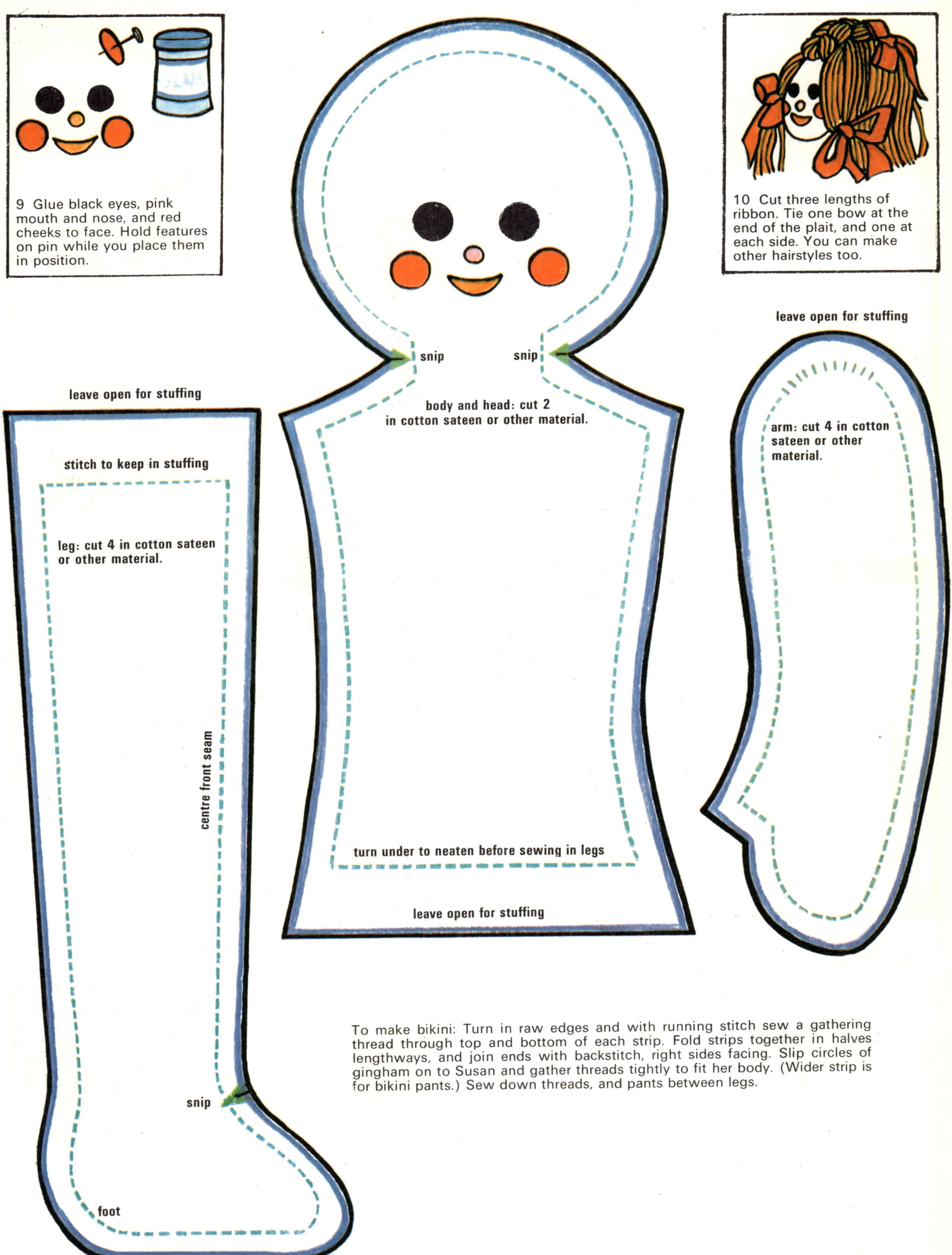

To make bikini: Turn in raw edges and with running stitch sew a gathering thread through top and bottom of each strip. Fold strips together in halves lengthways, and join ends with backstitch, right sides facing. Slip circles of gingham on to Susan and gather threads tightly to fit her body. (Wider strip is for bikini pants.) Sew down threads, and pants between legs.

Susan's Wardrobe

A glamorous teenage doll like black eyed Sue is going to need lots of clothes. Use your own ideas and these basic patterns to make them.

You will need: coat 22in. × 9in. fun fur; 1yd. folded $\frac{1}{2}$in.-wide braid; *blouse* 18in. × 6in. thin material; press stud; *hat* 8in. × 8in. fun fur; $\frac{1}{4}$yd. $\frac{1}{2}$in.-wide braid; *cape* 20in. × 7in. material; press stud; *kilt* strip of material 14in. × 3in.; press stud; safety pin; *boots* 12in. square felt; soft embroidery cotton; *long dress* 24in. × 12in. material; 1yd. narrow ribbon; soft embroidery cotton; scissors; pins; needles; tracing paper; felt tip pen; ruler.

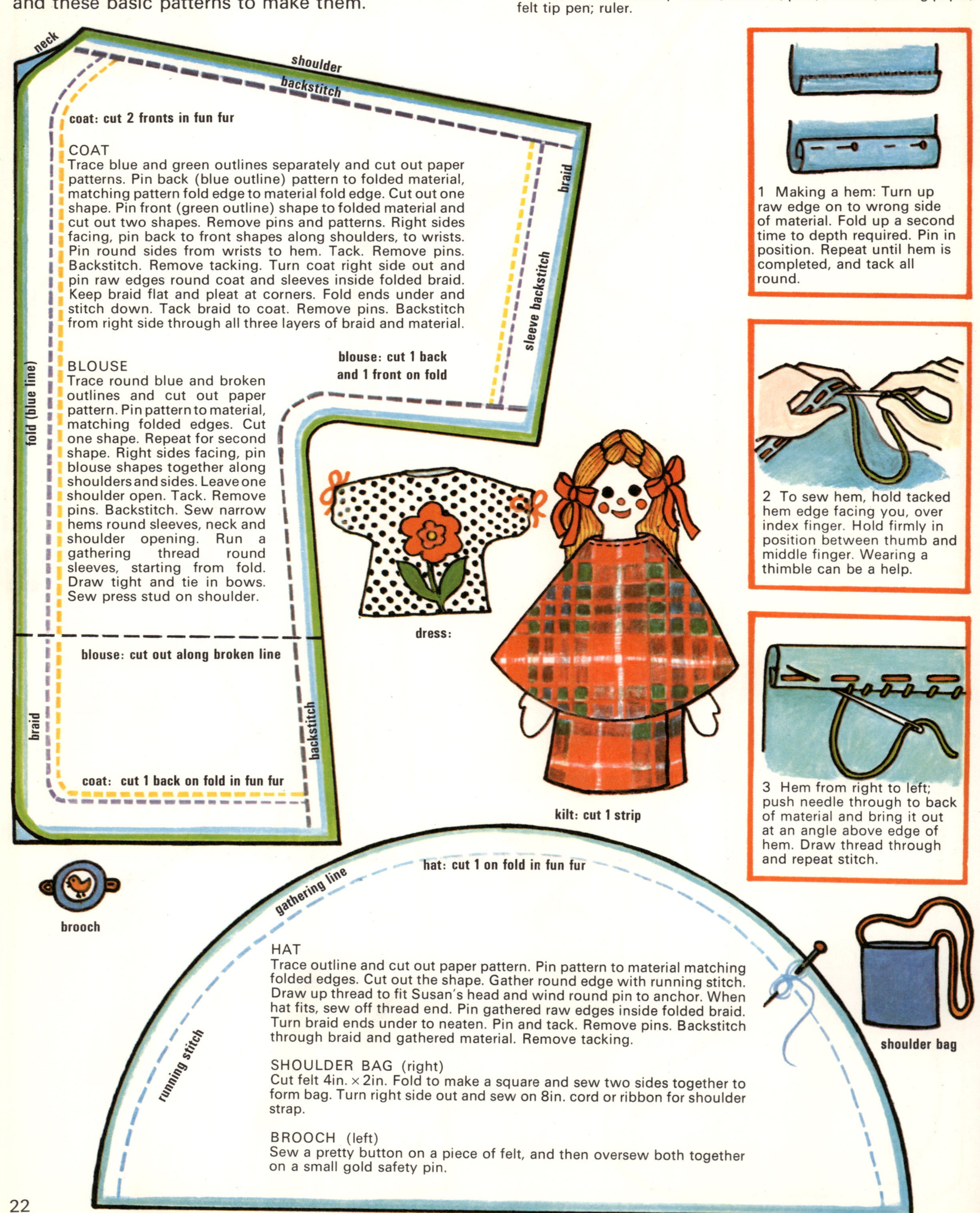

COAT
Trace blue and green outlines separately and cut out paper patterns. Pin back (blue outline) pattern to folded material, matching pattern fold edge to material fold edge. Cut out one shape. Pin front (green outline) shape to folded material and cut out two shapes. Remove pins and patterns. Right sides facing, pin back to front shapes along shoulders, to wrists. Pin round sides from wrists to hem. Tack. Remove pins. Backstitch. Remove tacking. Turn coat right side out and pin raw edges round coat and sleeves inside folded braid. Keep braid flat and pleat at corners. Fold ends under and stitch down. Tack braid to coat. Remove pins. Backstitch from right side through all three layers of braid and material.

BLOUSE
Trace round blue and broken outlines and cut out paper pattern. Pin pattern to material, matching folded edges. Cut one shape. Repeat for second shape. Right sides facing, pin blouse shapes together along shoulders and sides. Leave one shoulder open. Tack. Remove pins. Backstitch. Sew narrow hems round sleeves, neck and shoulder opening. Run a gathering thread round sleeves, starting from fold. Draw tight and tie in bows. Sew press stud on shoulder.

1 Making a hem: Turn up raw edge on to wrong side of material. Fold up a second time to depth required. Pin in position. Repeat until hem is completed, and tack all round.

2 To sew hem, hold tacked hem edge facing you, over index finger. Hold firmly in position between thumb and middle finger. Wearing a thimble can be a help.

3 Hem from right to left; push needle through to back of material and bring it out at an angle above edge of hem. Draw thread through and repeat stitch.

HAT
Trace outline and cut out paper pattern. Pin pattern to material matching folded edges. Cut out the shape. Gather round edge with running stitch. Draw up thread to fit Susan's head and wind round pin to anchor. When hat fits, sew off thread end. Pin gathered raw edges inside folded braid. Turn braid ends under to neaten. Pin and tack. Remove pins. Backstitch through braid and gathered material. Remove tacking.

SHOULDER BAG (right)
Cut felt 4in. × 2in. Fold to make a square and sew two sides together to form bag. Turn right side out and sew on 8in. cord or ribbon for shoulder strap.

BROOCH (left)
Sew a pretty button on a piece of felt, and then oversew both together on a small gold safety pin.

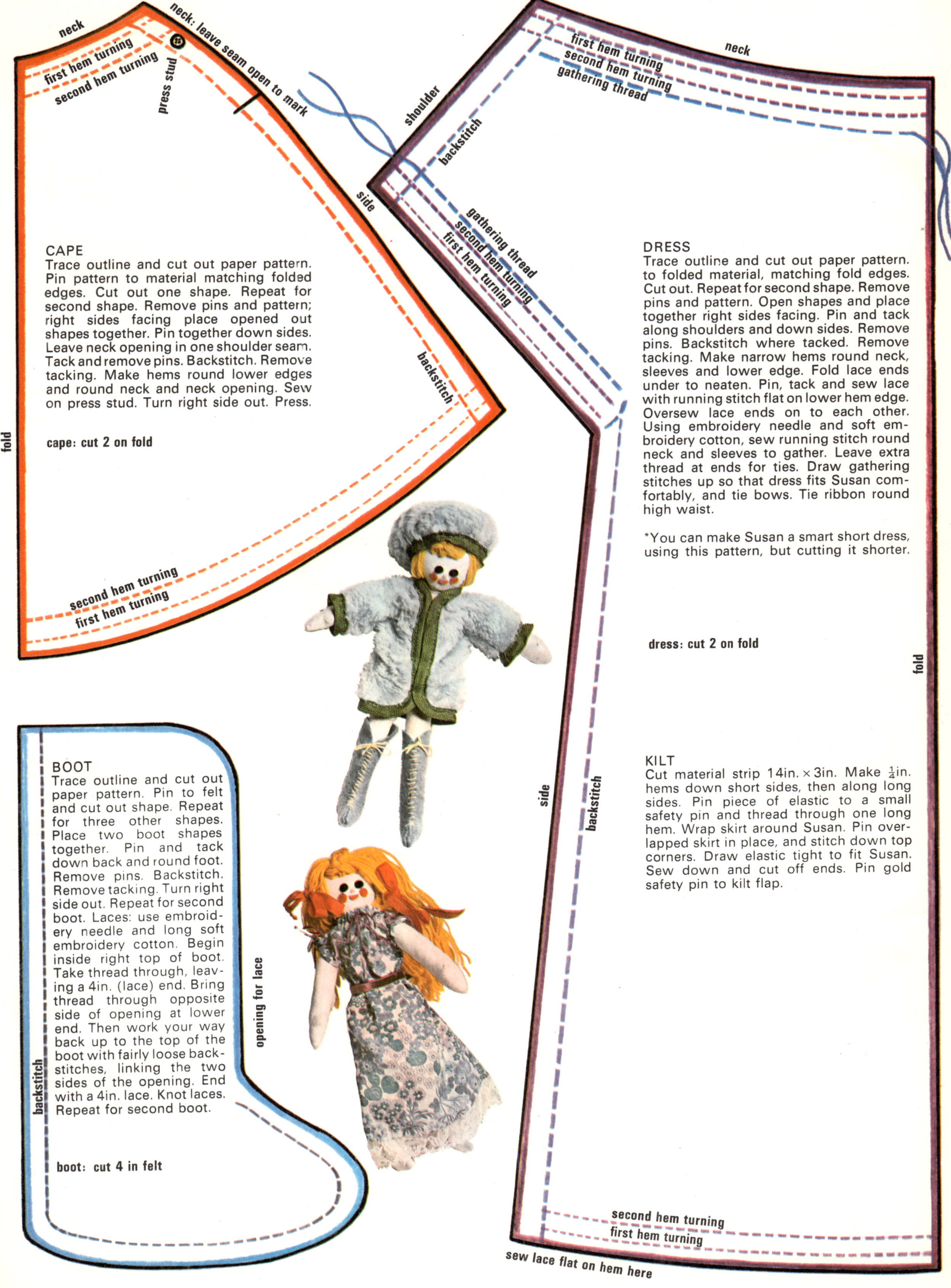

CAPE
Trace outline and cut out paper pattern. Pin pattern to material matching folded edges. Cut out one shape. Repeat for second shape. Remove pins and pattern; right sides facing place opened out shapes together. Pin together down sides. Leave neck opening in one shoulder seam. Tack and remove pins. Backstitch. Remove tacking. Make hems round lower edges and round neck and neck opening. Sew on press stud. Turn right side out. Press.

DRESS
Trace outline and cut out paper pattern. to folded material, matching fold edges. Cut out. Repeat for second shape. Remove pins and pattern. Open shapes and place together right sides facing. Pin and tack along shoulders and down sides. Remove pins. Backstitch where tacked. Remove tacking. Make narrow hems round neck, sleeves and lower edge. Fold lace ends under to neaten. Pin, tack and sew lace with running stitch flat on lower hem edge. Oversew lace ends on to each other. Using embroidery needle and soft embroidery cotton, sew running stitch round neck and sleeves to gather. Leave extra thread at ends for ties. Draw gathering stitches up so that dress fits Susan comfortably, and tie bows. Tie ribbon round high waist.

*You can make Susan a smart short dress, using this pattern, but cutting it shorter.

KILT
Cut material strip 14in. × 3in. Make $\frac{1}{4}$in. hems down short sides, then along long sides. Pin piece of elastic to a small safety pin and thread through one long hem. Wrap skirt around Susan. Pin overlapped skirt in place, and stitch down top corners. Draw elastic tight to fit Susan. Sew down and cut off ends. Pin gold safety pin to kilt flap.

BOOT
Trace outline and cut out paper pattern. Pin to felt and cut out shape. Repeat for three other shapes. Place two boot shapes together. Pin and tack down back and round foot. Remove pins. Backstitch. Remove tacking. Turn right side out. Repeat for second boot. Laces: use embroidery needle and long soft embroidery cotton. Begin inside right top of boot. Take thread through, leaving a 4in. (lace) end. Bring thread through opposite side of opening at lower end. Then work your way back up to the top of the boot with fairly loose backstitches, linking the two sides of the opening. End with a 4in. lace. Knot laces. Repeat for second boot.

Sewing Machine Talk

If you are able to use a sewing machine, you will be able to sew big, exciting things and have rapid results. A sewing machine is useful for making clothes, or large items such as the ladybird floor cushion, which would take a long time and be hard work to make by hand. Many modern machines can be adjusted so that they sew zig zag and embroidery stitches, as well as do all sorts of sewing jobs like hems.

Machine stitches should be strong and even on both sides of the material. If they are looped on one side, or break easily, consult a grown-up, and the machine instruction book. Sewing machine suppliers are usually very kind and will help with advice on sewing machines. If anything goes wrong, switch off the machine at once. Above all, do keep your fingers well away from the moving needle, and avoid accidents.

Although more people use electric sewing machines nowadays, hand machines like the black one in the picture are still often used. The material is clipped under the presser foot in the same way as an electric sewing machine, but you sit in front of the machine and wind a handle to move the needle up and down through the material. The small sewing machine is a battery-operated toy sewing machine. This will sew a lock stitch like a grown-up machine, but not usually through thick material.

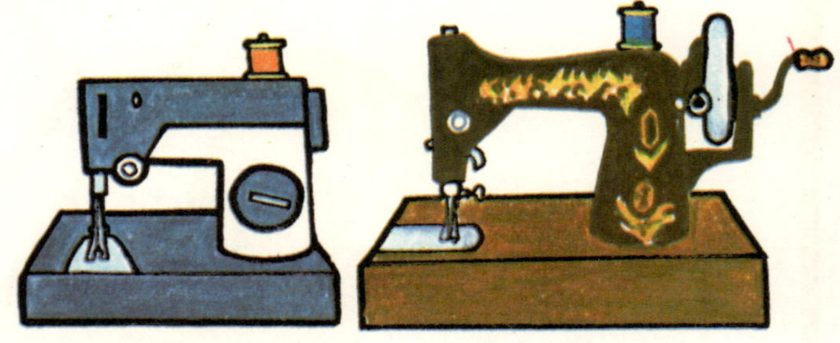

toy sewing machine **hand sewing machine**

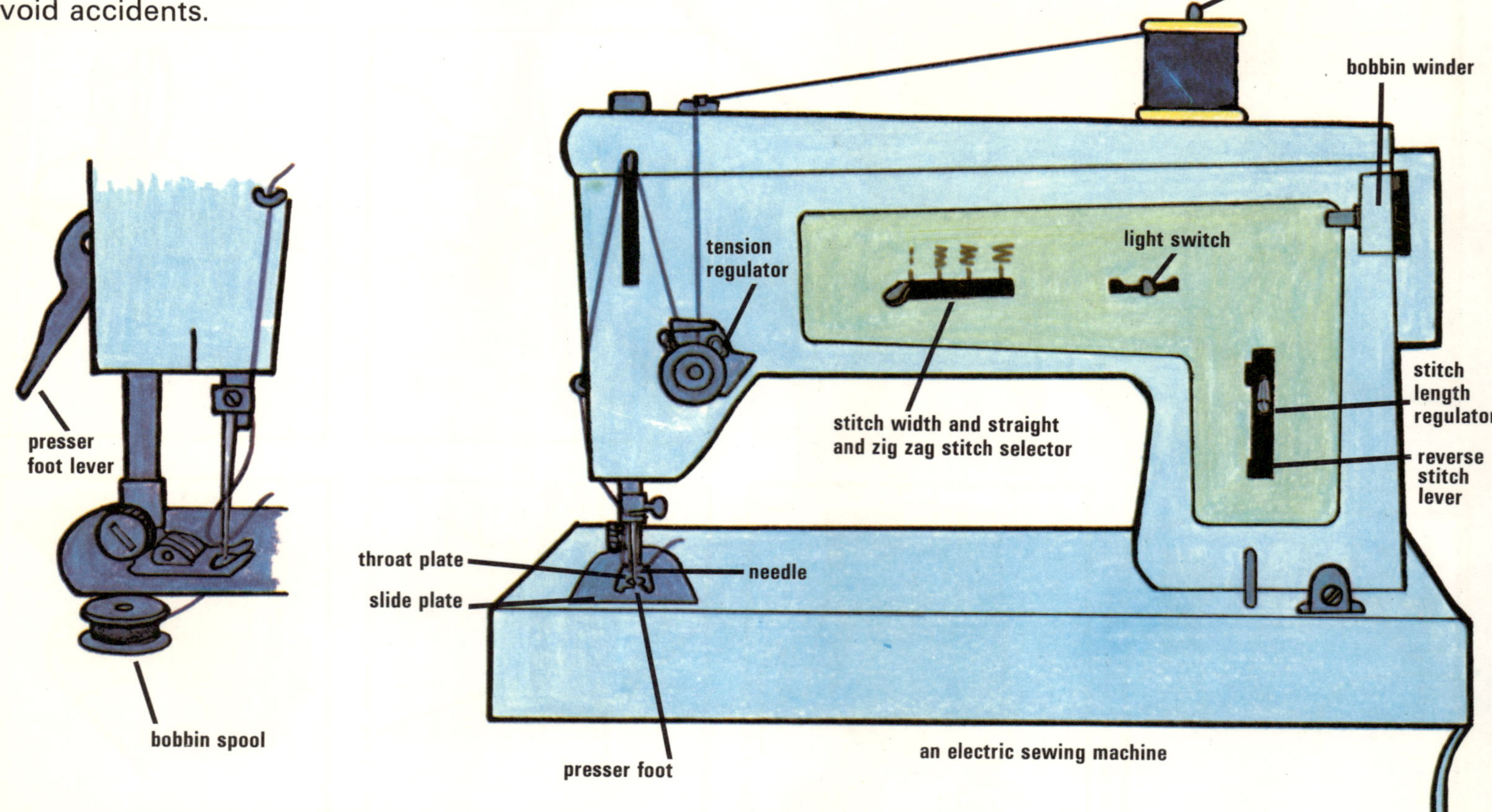

an electric sewing machine

Stitches are made by thread from above being linked with thread below the machine. This is called 'lock stitch'. The thread is placed on the **spool pin** and passed across hooks, and round the discs of the **tension regulator**. This is adjusted to keep the thread at the correct tension, so it does not snap when stitching. The thread end is passed through other hooks, and through the **machine needle**, from front to back. Meanwhile a **bobbin spool** has been filled with thread on the **bobbin winder**. The **bobbin spool** is put in the **bobbin race** under the machine needle, and the thread drawn back at the side, in a small groove. The **needle** is wound down to draw up the bobbin thread through a hole in the **throat plate**. The **slide plate** goes over the bobbin. When the material is placed under the **presser foot**, a springy clip behind the machine called the **presser foot lever** is pressed down to clip the **presser foot** on to the material. When you wish to draw out the material, the **presser foot lever** is lifted to raise the **presser foot**. Modern sewing machines often enable you to choose between straight and zig zag stitching. You select these on the **straight or zig zag stitch selector panel** as well as the **stitch width**. Stitch length is selected on the **stitch length regulator**. Reverse with **reverse stitch lever**.

Foot control: pressed by foot to control working needle

Sit comfortably at the right height. Have a good light to sew by.

Sewing machines usually have attachments or adjustments which enable you to do many sewing jobs more easily and rapidly. A special hemmer foot will sew narrow hems in one operation, and saves you turning and tacking the hem. Buttonholes can be sewn on some machines. Getting to know how to use every part of the machine is fun, and saves work. The machine booklet will tell you how to use the attachments, or ask a grown-up.

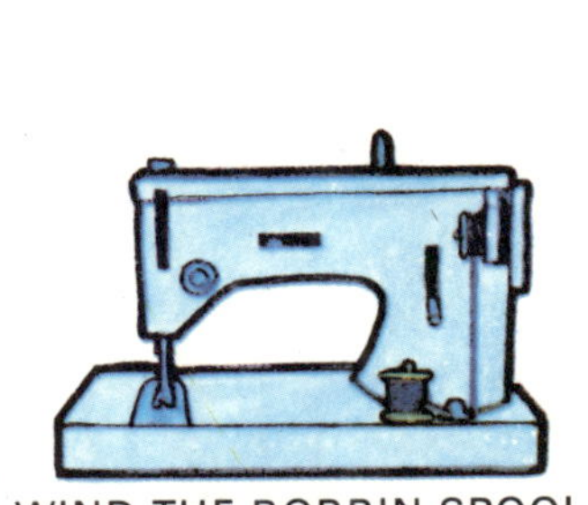

WIND THE BOBBIN SPOOL
1 Wind thread round bobbin spool a few times, and clip spool into winder. Fill with thread following booklet instructions.

THREAD THE MACHINE
2 The instruction booklet will show you how to thread your machine. Alternatively, ask for help from an adult or at the sewing machine shop.

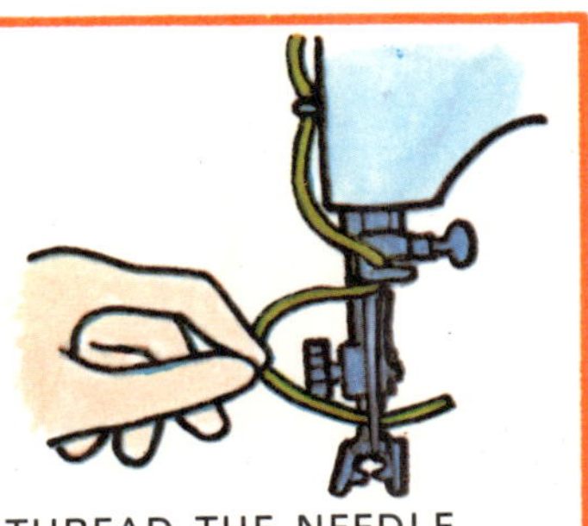

THREAD THE NEEDLE
3 The machine needle is usually threaded from left to right. Trim the end, moisten the thread and pass through the needle.

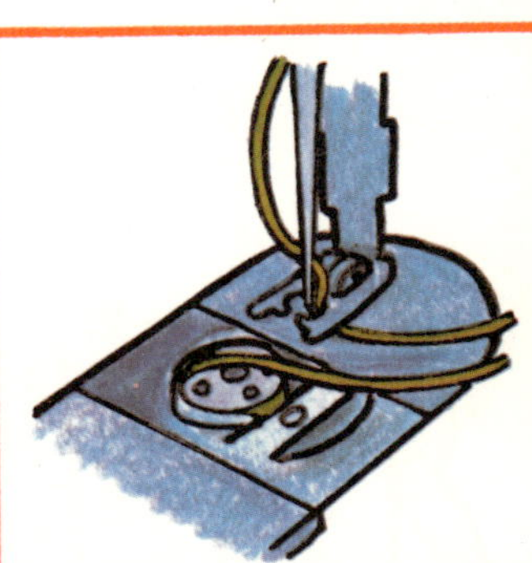

PICK UP BOBBIN THREAD
4 Put in threaded bobbin. Lower threaded needle and draw up bobbin thread.

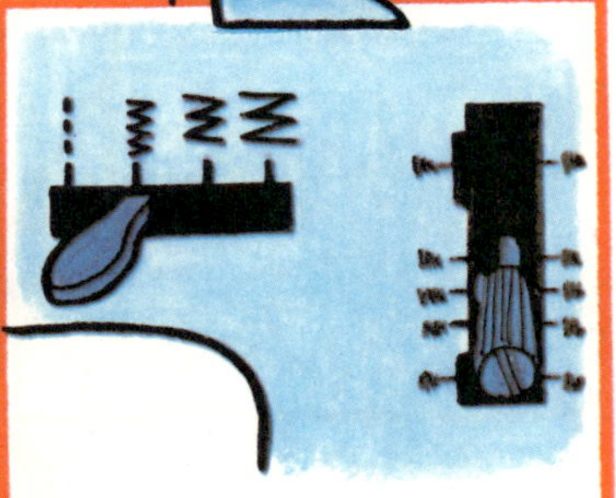

ADJUST STITCHES
5 Select kind of stitch required—i.e. straight or zig zag. Alter stitch length and width if necessary.

TEST THE STITCHES
6 No matter how familiar you become with using a sewing machine, it is always wise to test stitches on spare material before machining.

BEGIN TO SEW
7 Place material under presser foot. Clip presser foot lever down so foot grips material. Switch on or wind handle to start.

SEW A STRAIGHT LINE
8 Follow edge of presser foot or guide lines on throat plate for straight stitching.

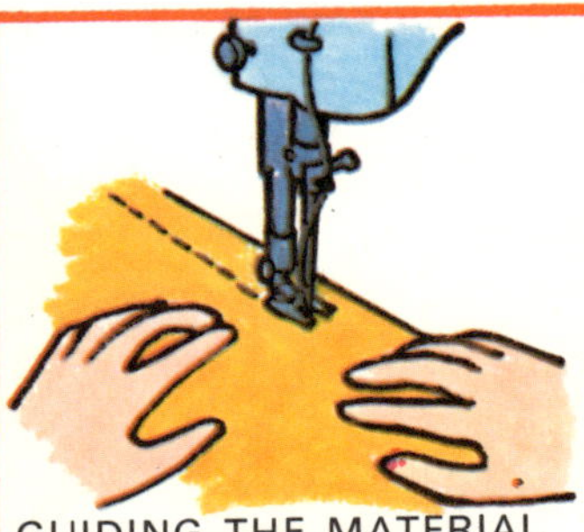

GUIDING THE MATERIAL
9 Guide the material under the presser foot with your hands, but don't push or pull it. Keep your fingers away from the needle!

CORNERS AND CURVES
10 Corners: stop at corner with needle down. Lift foot, turn material. Lower foot. Continue stitching. Curves: Guide material round gently while you sew.

FINISHING OFF
11 At the end of your sewing, reverse the stitches for a short distance and snip off thread.

SEWING MACHINE HINTS
12 Sewing machine needles come in different sizes, and you need to have the right size to suit the thickness of the material, as well as the right stitch length. A fine needle and small stitch are suitable for thin material, and thicker needle and long stitch for heavy weight material. Stretch material needs a stretch stitch if possible. Oil the machine lightly as instructed in the machine booklet, with the correct oil. Wipe away the surplus.

Badges and Motifs

With scraps of material and felt, you can make your own badges and motifs to sew on your clothes. Badges of all shapes and sizes, sewn to your jeans trousers, or your denim jacket will liven up your clothes no end, and are great fun. Motifs are slightly different. They are cut-out material shapes stitched to clothes in pictures. Our raspberry ice-cream cornet is a motif. You could have strawberries or a ship. Motifs can be embroidered, too.

You will need: Sam the Cat badge fawn felt $4\frac{1}{2}$in. × 5in.; scraps green felt; pink, orange, black, soft embroidery thread; *Moon and Stars badge* navy blue felt; yellow and pale blue soft embroidery cotton; *Sailing Boat badge* turquoise felt $3\frac{1}{2}$in. × $3\frac{1}{2}$in.; scraps white, navy blue felt; yellow and red soft embroidery cotton. *Forget-me-not Heart badge* bright green felt $4\frac{1}{2}$in. × $4\frac{1}{2}$in.; red felt for heart; green, blue and yellow soft embroidery cotton. *Someone has Eyes on You spectacles badge* white, orange and black felt; blue soft embroidery cotton. *Raspberry Ice-Cream motif* 6in. × 5in. raspberry pink satin for ice cream; 6in. × 4in. yellow satin for cornet; matching thread. Scissors; pins; needles; tracing paper; felt tip pen.

To appliqué shapes to material; trace and cut out paper patterns. Pin to material and cut out shapes. Tack in position carefully, background shapes before foreground shapes, keeping them flat on the garment. Then sew them on to the material round the edges, using either embroidered or machine satin stitch, or other embroidery stitches. Firm material which does not fray easily is best for appliqué.

MOON AND STARS
1 Draw round a jar on felt and cut out. Transfer moon and stars shapes. Embroider stars with straight, and moon with diagonal, satin stitch.

SAILING BOAT
2 Trace outlines separately, and cut out shapes in coloured felt. Sew on boat with running stitch. Sew flag in satin stitch.

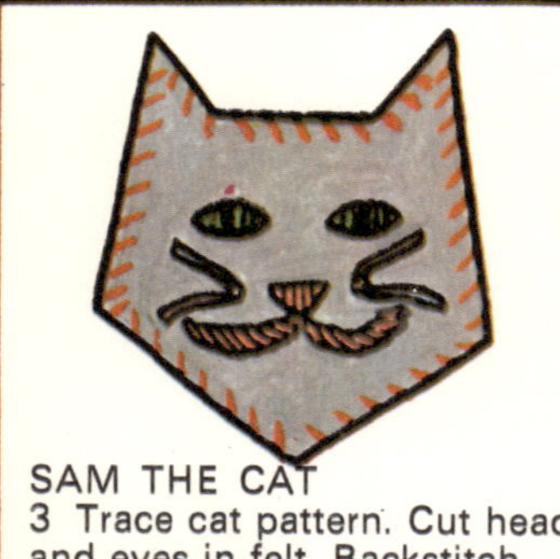

SAM THE CAT
3 Trace cat pattern. Cut head and eyes in felt. Backstitch eyes in place. Work nose in satin stitch and mouth in stem stitch; oversew edges.

FORGET-ME-NOT HEART
4 Trace and cut out heart and square in felt. Sew on heart and borders with fly stitch. Forget-me-nots are lazy-daisies.

To make badges, trace outline of badge, and appliqué shapes separately. To transfer embroidery designs, you will need dressmaker's carbon paper; a board; four drawing pins, a ball-point pen and tailor's chalk.

Pin the badge tracing over the dressmaker's carbon, and place over the material on the board. Pin through all layers at corners. Draw round outlines of traced pattern shapes pressing firmly to transfer the lines.

When the tracing is complete, remove the tracing and carbon. Draw over faint lines in tailor's chalk.

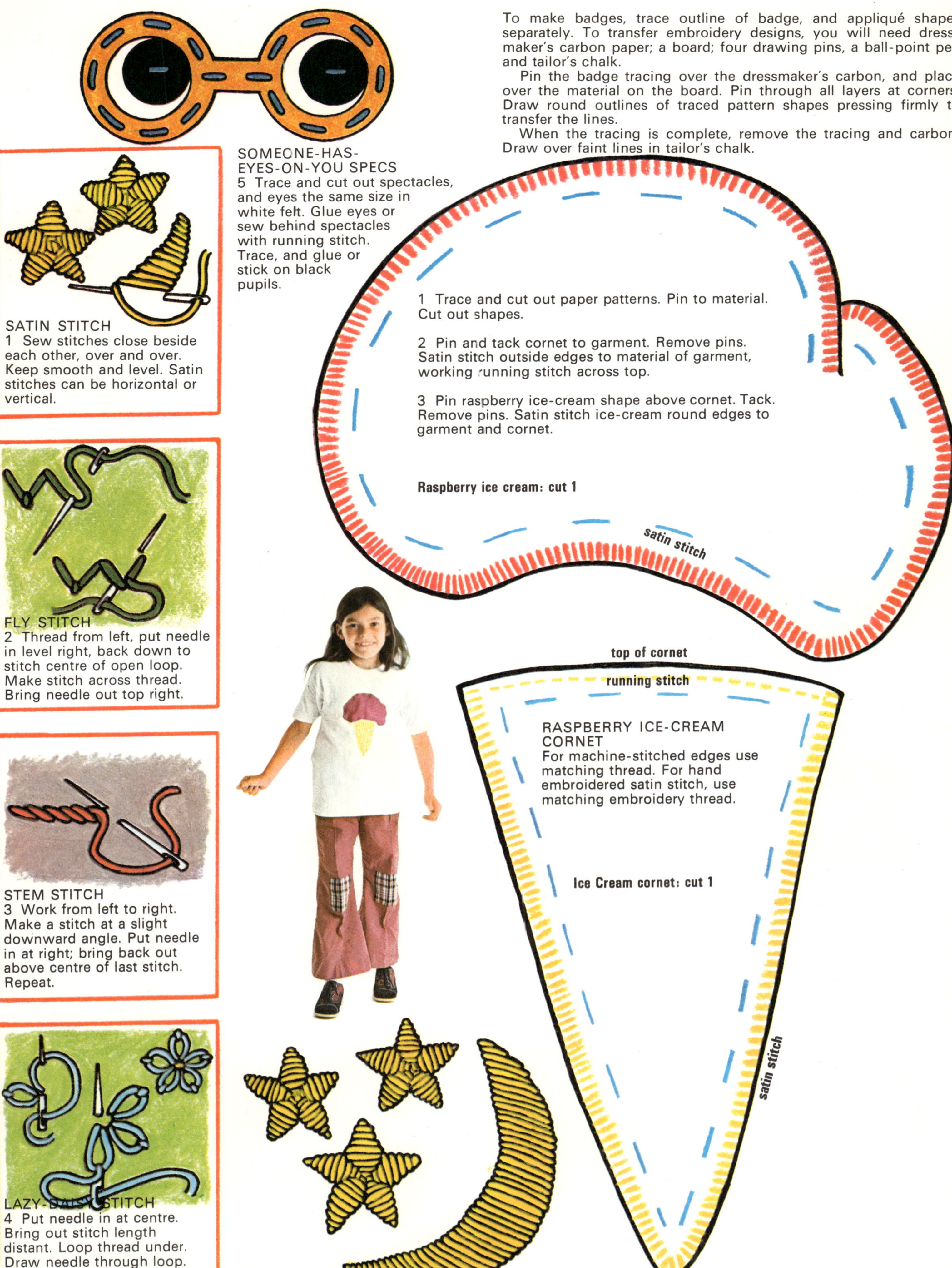

SATIN STITCH
1 Sew stitches close beside each other, over and over. Keep smooth and level. Satin stitches can be horizontal or vertical.

FLY STITCH
2 Thread from left, put needle in level right, back down to stitch centre of open loop. Make stitch across thread. Bring needle out top right.

STEM STITCH
3 Work from left to right. Make a stitch at a slight downward angle. Put needle in at right; bring back out above centre of last stitch. Repeat.

LAZY-DAISY STITCH
4 Put needle in at centre. Bring out stitch length distant. Loop thread under. Draw needle through loop. Stitch over loop. Repeat.

SOMEONE-HAS-EYES-ON-YOU SPECS
5 Trace and cut out spectacles, and eyes the same size in white felt. Glue eyes or sew behind spectacles with running stitch. Trace, and glue or stick on black pupils.

1 Trace and cut out paper patterns. Pin to material. Cut out shapes.

2 Pin and tack cornet to garment. Remove pins. Satin stitch outside edges to material of garment, working running stitch across top.

3 Pin raspberry ice-cream shape above cornet. Tack. Remove pins. Satin stitch ice-cream round edges to garment and cornet.

RASPBERRY ICE-CREAM CORNET
For machine-stitched edges use matching thread. For hand embroidered satin stitch, use matching embroidery thread.

Revamping Old Clothes

There are many things you can do to change your old clothes into new. A faded, torn or worn looking garment, given a few patches or dyed a different colour, can be quite transformed. What a good way of getting something new to wear when one's clothes budget is looking rather thin.

Here are some ideas to start you thinking about the fashion possibilities in some of the abandoned clothes in your wardrobe. A school blouse dyed and cheered up with a big kipper tie, or a tartan ruffle. Revamped jeans. A vest from a tee-shirt. How about changing the elbow threadbare sleeves in an old favourite sweater for contrasting new ones? You can use the old sleeve for the pattern. The same goes for trouser panels. And there are lots more ideas.

You will need: Jeans, for two flares, two pockets, one seat patch—about $\frac{1}{2}$yd. 36in.-wide material; *vest* 3yd. red bias binding; 1$\frac{1}{4}$yd. yellow bias binding; 4$\frac{1}{2}$in. yellow ric-rac braid; buttons; *kipper tie blouse* purple dye; two pieces material each 14in. long × 8$\frac{1}{2}$in. wide; repeat once in taffeta; two press studs; *ruffled blouse* red dye; 18in. × 4$\frac{1}{2}$in. ribbon or plaid; 1$\frac{1}{2}$yd. broderie anglaise; 1yd. narrow black velvet ribbon; scissors; pins; needles; tape measure; felt tip pen; tracing paper; ruler.

To insert flares in jeans legs, unpick hems a short distance from seam then unpick seams to knees. To do this, insert the sharp point of unpick-ing tool between seam under stitches, and cut stitch.

INSERT FLARES IN JEANS
1 Spread open unpicked seams. Place paper under and pin in position. Draw outline of flare with hem allowance.

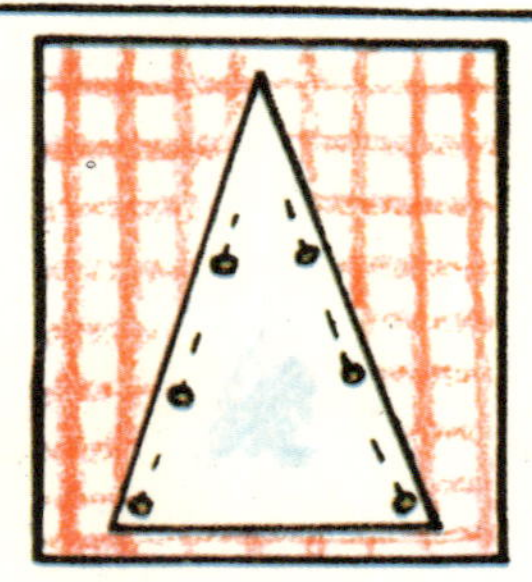

2 Cut out paper pattern and pin to material. Cut out two flare shapes.

3 Turn jeans inside out. Pin flare into leg. Tack. Remove pins. Machine along tacking. Hem bottom edge. Repeat for second flare.

4 Remove tacking. Turn jeans right side out. Press flares and hems carefully.

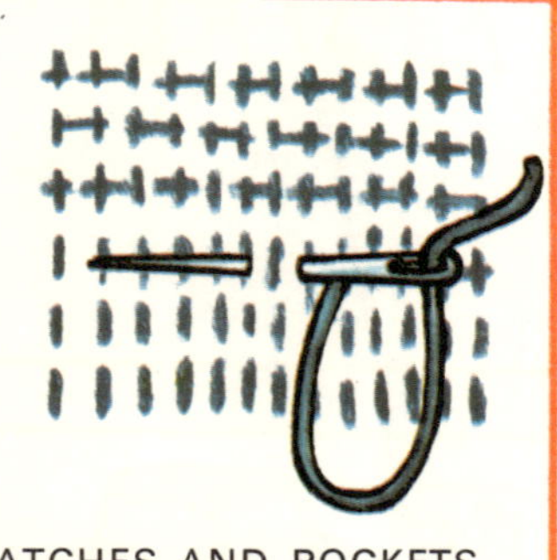

PATCHES AND POCKETS
1 Darn worn part with rows of running stitches, worked across first and then down.

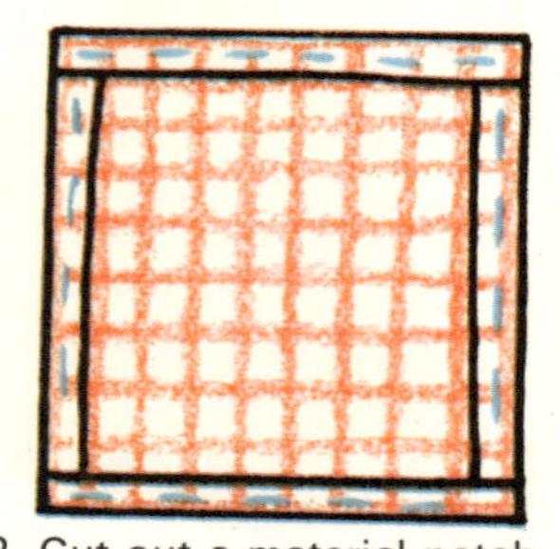

2 Cut out a material patch to cover the darn. Add hem allowances. Turn under raw edges, pin and tack over darn.

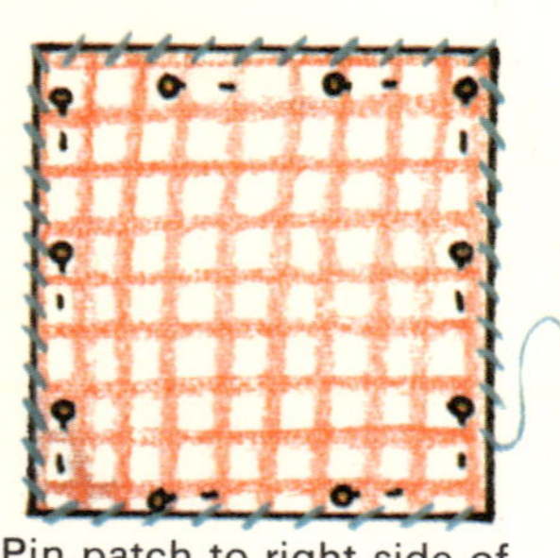

3 Pin patch to right side of material over darn. Tack. Remove pins. Hem or machine patch to jeans all round.

4 To make a patch pocket; hem at top edge. Pin, tack and sew to jeans, with top left open.

Front and back view of jeans with new flares, pockets and seat patch.

Take an old school blouse. Wash it. Dye it purple, following the dye maker's instructions. Now give it a kipper tie. Trace outline and cut out paper pattern first.

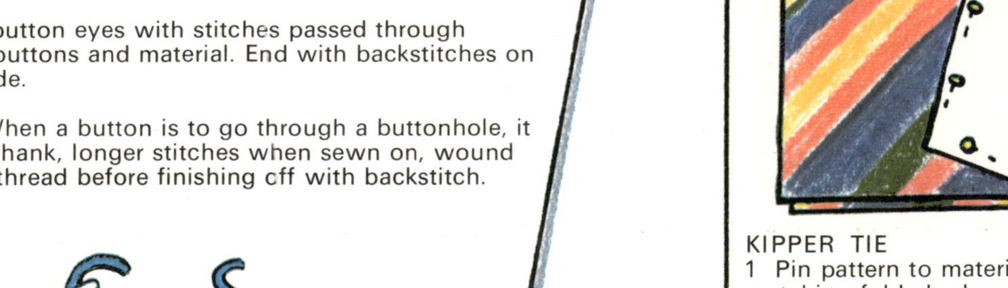

Sew on button eyes with stitches passed through holes in buttons and material. End with backstitches on wrong side.

Shank: When a button is to go through a buttonhole, it needs a shank, longer stitches when sewn on, wound with the thread before finishing off with backstitch.

VEST
1 Renovate a tee-shirt. Cut away the collar and sleeves to make a vest shape. Trim neatly.

2 Sew red bias binding round neck and armholes.

Spaceman: make from folded yellow bias strip with ric-rac ariel, machined to vest.

Strips: Spaceman, 26in.; Nose, 5in.; mouth, 2in.; ariel, T shaped. 2 button eyes.

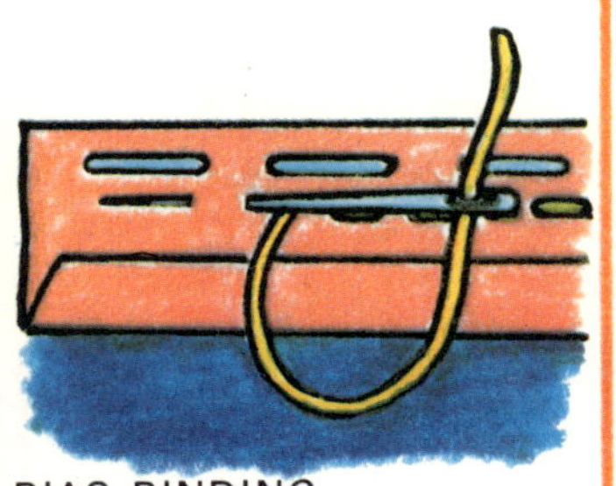

BIAS BINDING
1 Open one side of binding. Place against right side of material, raw edges together. Pin and tack. Backstitch or machine in crease.

2 Turn binding on to wrong side of material. Pin, and tack above stitch line. Remove pins. Hem, but so that stitches do not show through.

Kipper Tie: cut 2 in material, 1 interlining;

Extend line to 13in.

Extend line to same length as other line

FOLD

KIPPER TIE
1 Pin pattern to material, matching folded edges. Cut two ties and one interlining.

2 Pin lining and tie shapes together, right sides facing. Tack and machine round edge except for top. Turn right side out. Pleat top.

3 Cut a strip of the material 7in. × $3\frac{1}{2}$in., turn in and tack raw edges. Fold strip round pleated top of tie. Stitch ends over each other at tie back.

4 Sew press stud tops on to back of tie knot. Sew press stud undersides under collar. Fix tie to blouse.

PLAID RUFFLED BLOUSE
Dye blouse scarlet. Use 18in. × $4\frac{1}{2}$in.-wide plaid ribbon or hemmed tartan. Trim with lace or broderie anglaise. Gather down the centre. Stitch to blouse front from collar, beside button-holes. Add long stringed black velvet ribbon Maverick tie-bow.

centre front fold

Smock Top

Hand smocking is a delightful way of decorating a garment. It is embroidery stitches of different kinds sewn over gathered material.

In the old days, country workers wore smocks embroidered with the badge of their work, such as a cart wheel for a carter. What would your badge be? Something to do with your favourite hobby perhaps, such as a pair of scissors! You could work some embroidery on the shoulders of this smock top.

We have shown you how to do two types of smocking stitch here. If you want to know how to do some more stitches, you could borrow a book about it from the library.

extend lines beyond blue and green arrows until pattern is desired length

centre back fold

You will need: $1\frac{1}{4}$yd. check gingham 36in. wide. (Gingham with $\frac{3}{16}$in. check is a good size square pattern to learn smocking.) 4yds. bias binding; thread to match gingham and other thread to match binding; a skein of stranded embroidery thread; two press studs; scissors; pins; large and small needles; a thimble; a tape measure; tracing paper; felt tip pen; ruler; pencil.

If you wish to smock on plain material, it is possible to buy transfers marked with dots, which you iron on, as markers.

1 Decide on length of smock. Cut tracing paper to this length. Trace patterns separately. The blue outline is for the front pattern; the green outline for the back pattern.

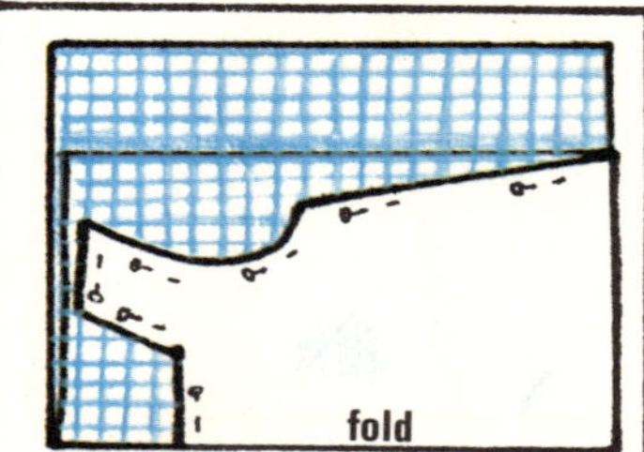

2 Fold material carefully, matching checks, to cut out shapes without wasting material. Place fold edge of pattern against folded edge of material. Cut out one back and one front.

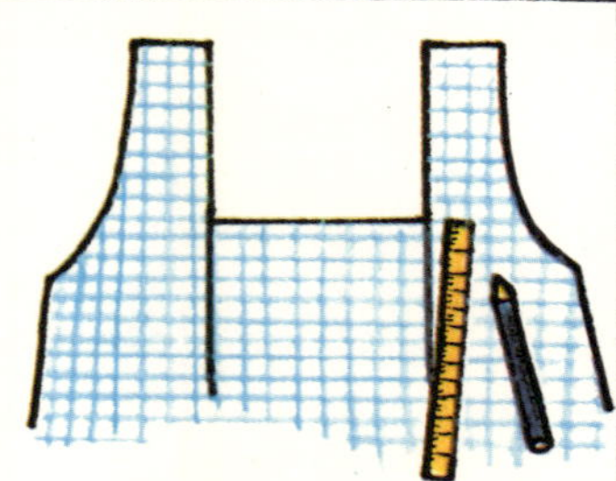

3 Open out shapes. Rule two pencil lines $3\frac{1}{2}$in. long on wrong side of front as shown. Stitch horizontal gathering lines of running stitch between them (see below).

4 Gather up front smocking panel to 4in. wide. Work stitches as shown on this and the next page.

sew bias binding all round lower edge of smock top

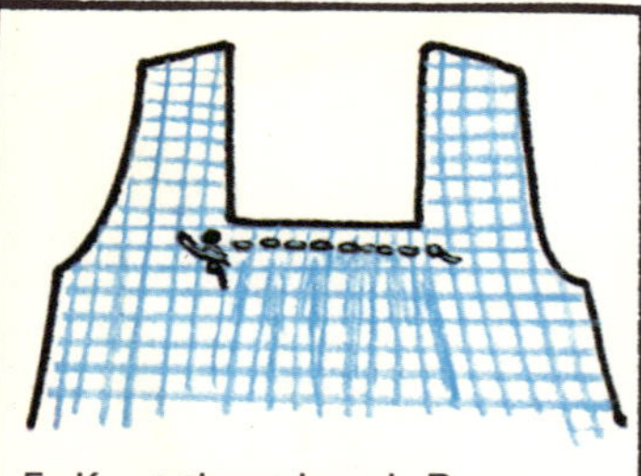

5 Knot thread end. Run a line of running stitch to gather back of smock neckline. Draw thread to gather to 4in. wide neckline. Wind thread round a pin to anchor it.

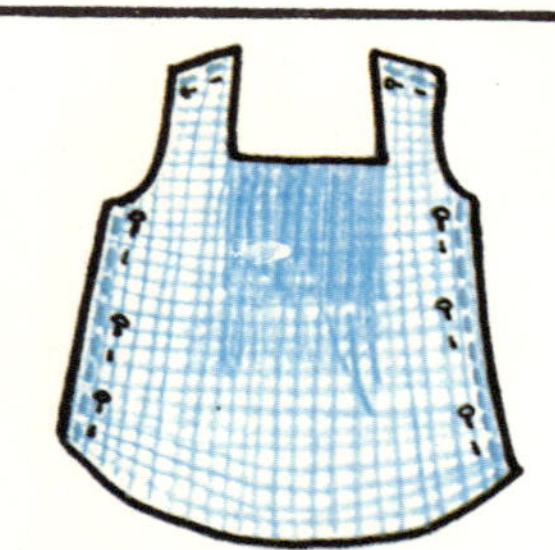

6 With right sides facing, pin front to back. Tack and remove pins. Machine or backstitch together down sides and across right shoulder only.

7 Sew bias binding round neck and open shoulder edges, and also round armholes and lower hem edges.

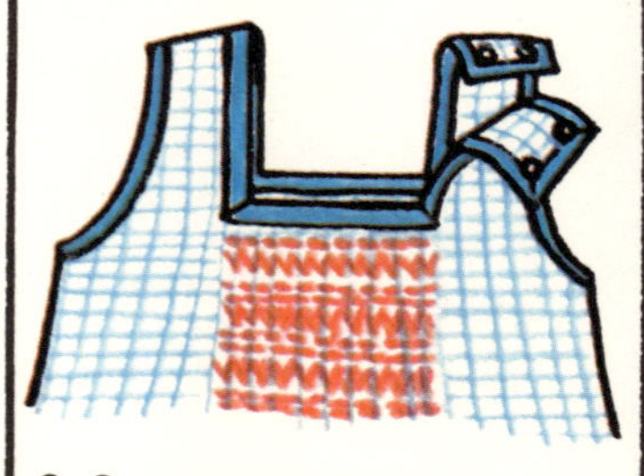

8 Sew two press studs inside open shoulder to fasten—underside of the press studs on to back right side, and tops to wrong side front.

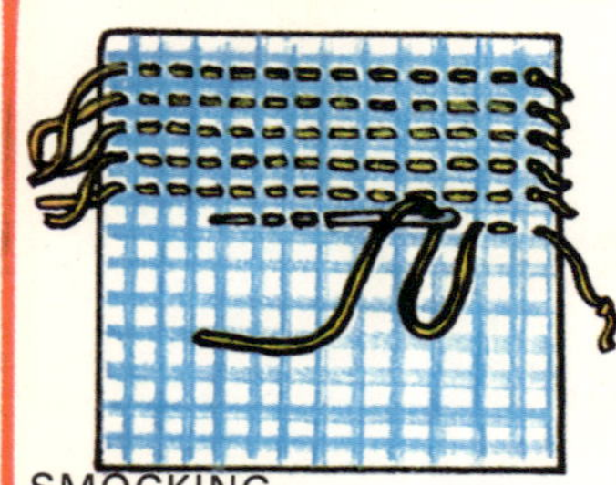

SMOCKING

1 Run gathering rows on wrong side. Use long thread with knot in end. Push needle in and out behind dark lines, so stitches are directly beneath each other.

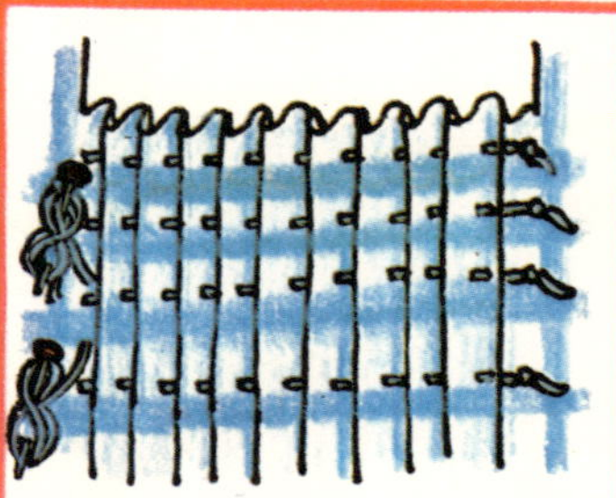

2 Carefully draw threads tighter so pleats form, to required width of smocking. Wind ends round pins to anchor, two threads at a time.

3 Thread an embroidery needle with embroidery thread. Knot end. Begin smocking at back (right) of material with two backstitches.

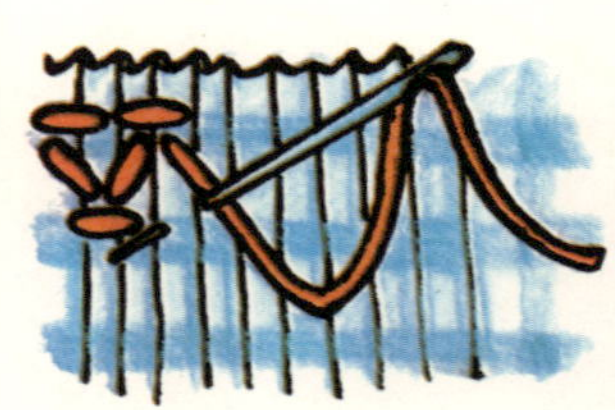

4 Bring thread through to front of material. Thread is now at left of row. Stitch from left to right evenly across gathers.

extend lines beyond blue and green arrows to desired length **side** **½in. side seam allowed** **backstitch or straight machine stitch**

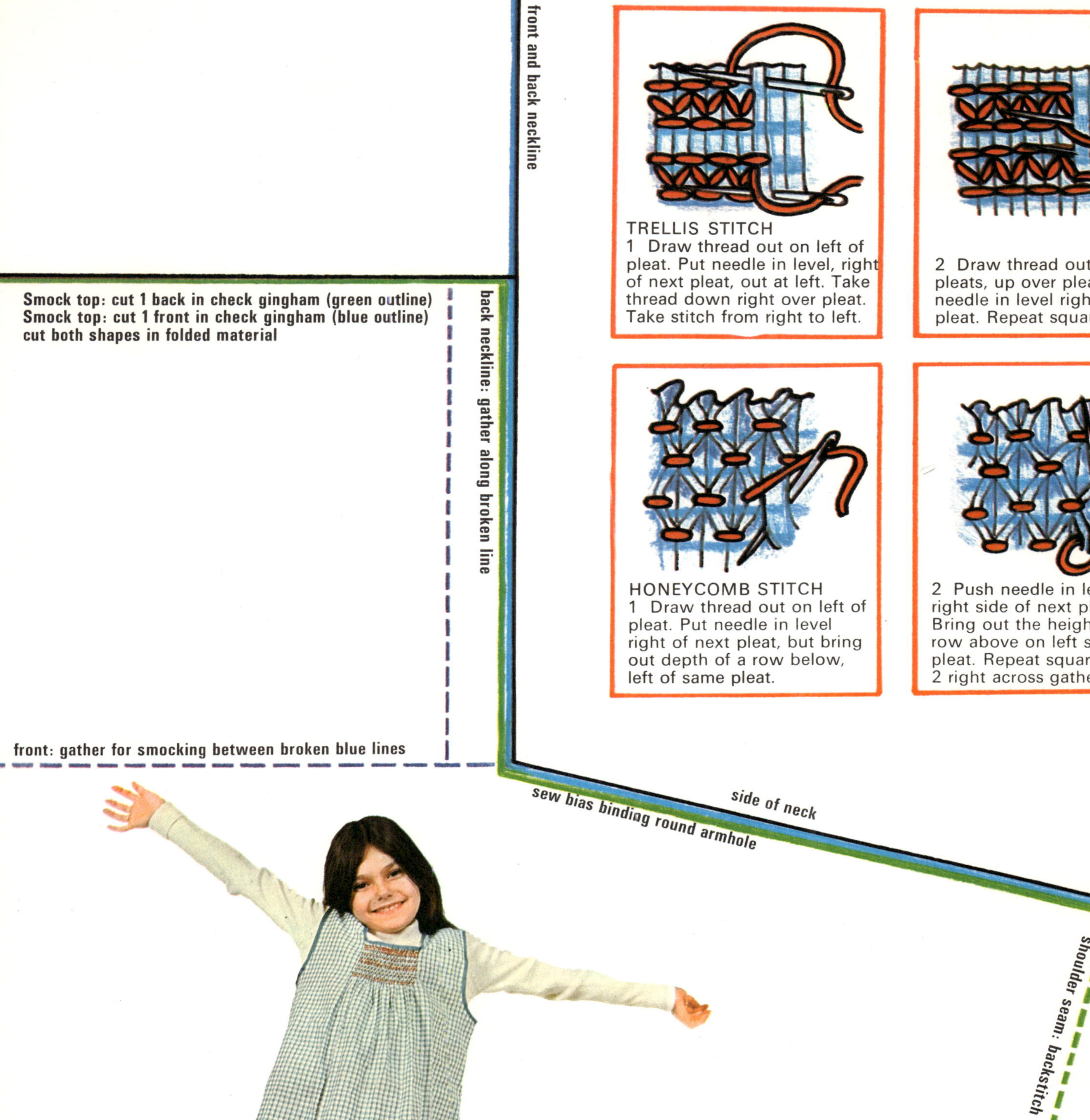

Smock top: cut 1 back in check gingham (green outline)
Smock top: cut 1 front in check gingham (blue outline)
cut both shapes in folded material

TRELLIS STITCH

1 Draw thread out on left of pleat. Put needle in level, right of next pleat, out at left. Take thread down right over pleat. Take stitch from right to left.

2 Draw thread out between pleats, up over pleat. Put needle in level right to left of pleat. Repeat squares 1 and 2.

HONEYCOMB STITCH

1 Draw thread out on left of pleat. Put needle in level right of next pleat, but bring out depth of a row below, left of same pleat.

2 Push needle in level on right side of next pleat. Bring out the height of a row above on left side of pleat. Repeat squares 1 and 2 right across gathering.

Tie-dye a Headscarf

Tie-dyeing is an exciting way of putting your own colour printing into materials, using simple and inexpensive methods. It is done by tying material with string, or pleating and knotting it in different ways, then dyeing it, in one or more colours. It is easy to do, if you follow the maker's instructions for using the dye, and quite exceptional fun.

Having chosen your dye colours, prepare them in suitable old utensils, and then get the material you want to tie-and-dye ready. New material should be washed before dyeing to remove dressing. Try tying a stone in the middle of a shirt and twist the material above it, binding it with string tightly. Dye it, retie it with the first tie still in place, and dye it again. When it's done, you will have made lovely patterns.

A tie dyed headscarf like this would make a lovely present.

TO MAKE HEADSCARF
1 Cut out a square of material 30in. × 30in. for scarf. Make narrow hems on four sides of scarf.

You will need: for Stone-tied scarf lawn 30in. × 30in.; thread; 12 small clean pebbles in mixed sizes; fine string; two dye colours (we used turquoise first and burgundy red second); utensils for dyeing as suggested by the dye leaflet. (Keep exclusively for this use in future.)
Marbled scarf 30in. × 30in. white seersucker; thread; fine string; two colours of dye (yellow first and turquoise second); dye utensils; scissors; pins; needles.

2 Take about six pebbles. Put one inside the scarf and twist it tightly. Bind above with string and tie ends. Repeat for other pebbles.

3 Prepare first dye colour, and dye scarf tied with pebbles, following maker's instructions. Rinse well with pebbles still tied in.

4 Keep first pebbles tied in place, and twist and bind more pebbles in the spaces between them, so the scarf has lots of knobbly lumps.

5 Prepare the second dye colour, and dye the scarf again, this time with its double number of stones. Rinse well as before.

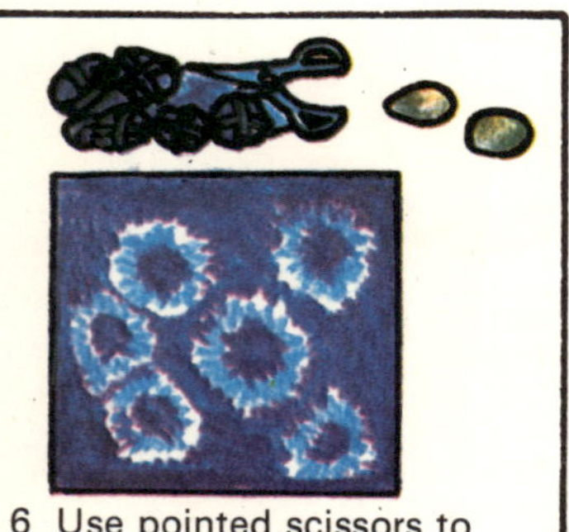

6 Use pointed scissors to cut strings and remove pebbles. Take care not to cut scarf. Rinse, dry and press scarf.

MARBLED HEADSCARF
1 Crumple scarf into a ball. Tie round with string a few times. Dye in first colour. Rinse with string still tied.

2 Bind more string over the tied scarf bundle, to add to the marbled effect. Dye in second colour. Rinse.

3 Using pointed scissors very carefully cut away strings. Open out scarf. Rinse, dry and press.

You will need: ½yd. calico 36in. wide (or other plain cotton material); ¾yd. 1in.-wide brown braid; thread; scissors; pins; needles; tracing paper; felt tip pen; ruler; soft pencil; sewing machine.
For dye-painting you will need: colours of dye—for pony, chestnut brown; for flowers yellow, Dylon cold dye is suitable. To go with each dye you will need a pack of Paintex or other similar fabric dye, including the dye fix. For the larger areas of the pony, have a ¼in.-wide ordinary household painting brush; for the small areas, a medium size paint box brush. A piece of card.

A Pony Bag

A new way of using dye, as paint to make permanent pictures and designs on material, has been made possible by the arrival of commercial packs for this purpose. When the contents of this pack are added to a cold dye, they fix the colour, so it will not run when washed, and thicken it to make it easy to use as paint.

Perhaps you would like to practise using it with this stencil pony . . . and make a useful bag!

1 Trace pony. To make stencil cut out tracing carefully to form a pony-shaped hole in the paper. Trace and cut out white parts separately.

2 Place pony stencil on one bag shape at the centre (allowing for top hem). Draw round inside cut-out. Add white area outlines.

3 Place card under the bag shape to protect underneath from dye. Paint dark areas of pony, leaving white unpainted. Brush on flowers.

TO MAKE BAG
4 When painted stencil is dry, place two bag shapes together, right sides facing. Pin and tack to join down sides and across lower edge. Remove pins. Machine, or backstitch together where tacked. Turn 1in. hem all round top edge. Machine or hem. Turn right side out. Cut two 14in. long pieces of braid. Turn under ends to neaten. Pin to front and back of bag. Handles should be about 4½in. from sides. Machine to bag at ends.

Blanket Stitch Jacket

The shapes that make this jacket—front, back, sleeves, pockets—are all edged with blanket stitch, then sewn together edge to edge. The picture instructions tell you how to do this, and how to embroider the wool flowers and sew on the wooden beads. It is all easy and great fun.

If you haven't got any brightly coloured felt, you could use, with permission, the good parts of an old blanket. If there is enough to spare you could even add a tasselled hood, and line it.

You will need: $1\frac{3}{4}$yd. 36in.-wide red felt, or material cut from a worn woven blanket, preferably wool. Approximately ten skeins of embroidery wool (two or three each in pale lime green, pale blue, mustard and leaf brown), 2 dozen wooden beads. Allow extra material and embroidery wool skeins for larger patterns. Scissors; a large needle; a darning needle; thimble; tape measure; tracing paper; ruler; felt tip pen.

To line the jacket, use the same amount of 36in.-wide silky material cut out in the same pattern shapes but with $\frac{3}{4}$in. seams allowed round all sides of each shape.

Turn in the edges of the lining shapes $\frac{3}{4}$in. on to the wrong side of the material. Pin and tack inside the jacket and sleeves when completed, matching lining edges to blanket stitch edges. Hem to jacket.

side

extend lines beyond arrows to pattern length desired

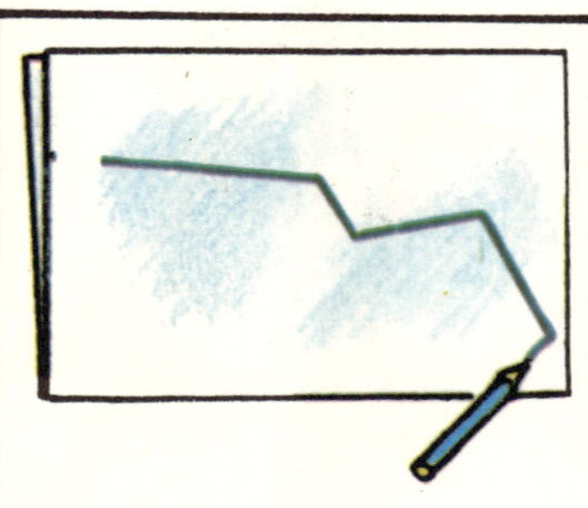

1 Fold tracing paper in half and place against fold edge of jacket back outline. Trace and cut out pattern. Repeat for sleeve and fronts.

2 Cut out paper patterns. Pin together and try on for fit. Pin to felt and cut out one back, two fronts and two sleeves.

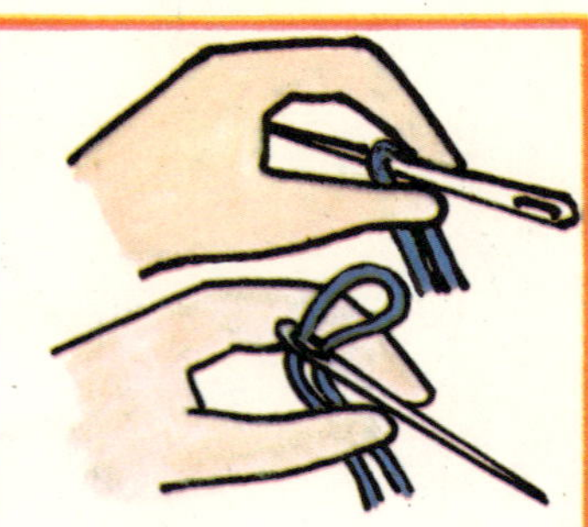

3 Double wool tightly over a wool darning needle. Pinch folded wool between fingers and press through needle eye. Draw end out.

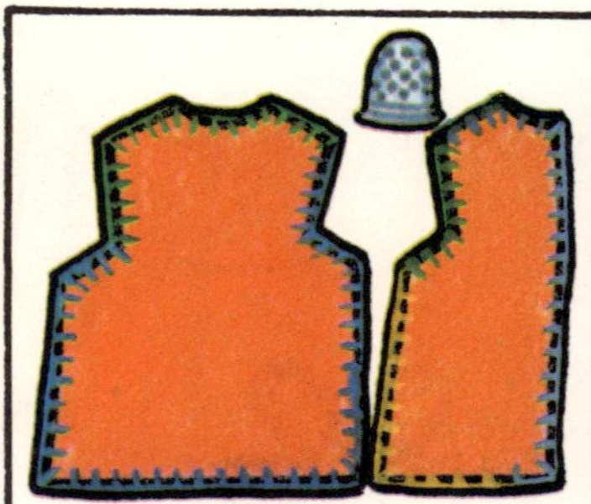

4 Wear your thimble, and using the wool threaded needle, sew large blanket stitches round all edges of jacket and sleeve shapes.

5 Place back and fronts flat on table, right side up with shoulders matching as shown. Oversew front to back along shoulders.

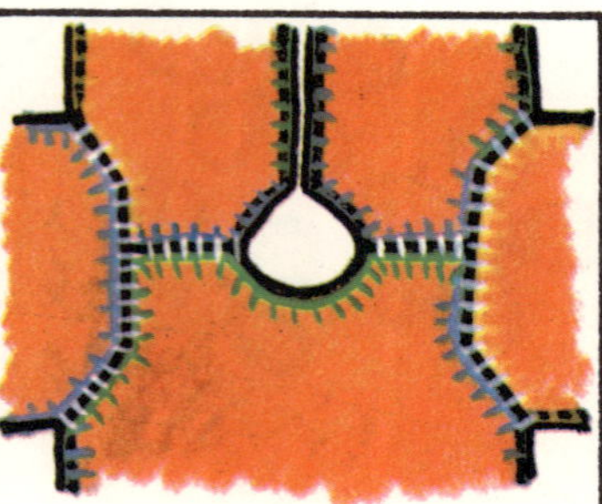

6 Still with jacket shapes flat on table, place sleeves so tops fit into armholes. Oversew together along tops and underarm angles.

7 Fold jacket so front and back including sleeves are wrong sides facing. Sew together down sleeve and side seams.

8 Draw a 6in. square of paper, and cut out. Pin to felt and cut out for pocket. Repeat for second pocket. Embroider as shown.

9 Sew wooden beads to centre of flowers. Begin at back of felt with a knot. Sew on beads with backstitches. End on wrong side securely.

10 Pin pockets in place on front of jacket, 1in. from lower edge, and $1\frac{1}{2}$in. from front edge. Tack. Remove pins and hem to jacket.

11 Make bead ties. Thread wool and knot end. Sew several times through first bead. Knot twice close above bead. Repeat for five more beads.

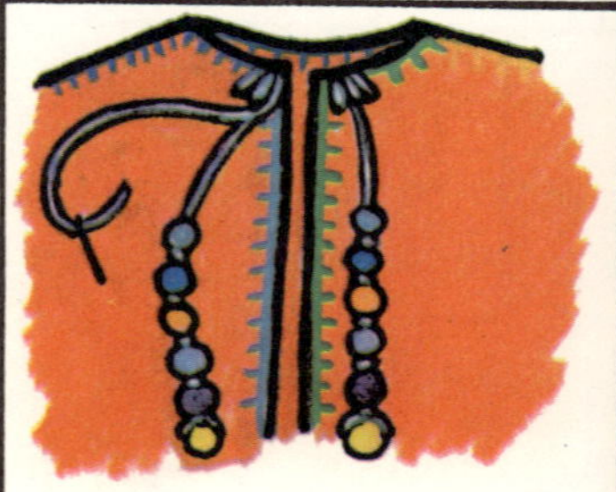

12 Repeat for second bead tie, then sew with 6in. long strings to front top corners at neck, with several oversewing stitches. Snip wool.

extend lines beyond arrows to pattern length desired

top
join to underarm along here
jacket front: cut 2 in red felt
underarm
side of armhole
shoulder
fold
jacket back: cut 1 in red felt
jacket sleeve: cut 2 in red felt
Embroider a star of backstitches in one or more colours of wool for flowers. Sew three beads at centre of large flower, one bead on small flower.
extend line beyond arrow to lengthen sleeve pattern if wished
sleeve seam
BLANKET STITCH
1 Work from left to right. Start with a knot at top back. Put needle in from front and bring out in front of thread above edge.
2 Take needle right through material, and draw out in front of thread which lies along top edge. Do not pull or pucker stitch.
3 To work corner: put needle in at bottom of last stitch. Bring out at corner. Secure with small extra stitch. Start next stitch at corner.
front neckline
back neckline
centre back fold
centre front opening

Moccasox

It isn't always easy to find just the design of slippers as attractive as you would like, and also comfortable to wear indoors, to slip on when getting out of bed in the morning, or after the bath.

One answer is—make some for yourself! These moccasin slippers, made of brightly coloured embroidered felt, are stitched on to soft and cosy bedsocks and have foam plastic innersoles glued underneath to make them firm underfoot. Cork soles are suitable, too. Tasselled laces keep them on comfortably. You could also make the moccasins separately, without the socks, for summer.

To shorten moccasin slippers, compare your size shoe to a size 4 (our size). Measure the difference in length, and when you have traced and cut out the paper slipper pattern, pleat it across the centre to remove the extra amount. Remember though, they should be roomy.

You will need: 1 pair of thick knit socks or bed socks to fit you comfortably; a pair of polythene foam plastic or cork innersoles in your own shoe size; $\frac{1}{4}$yd. 36in.-wide pink felt; 9in. squares moss green and peacock blue felt; or two pieces of each colour $4\frac{1}{2}$in. × $4\frac{1}{2}$in. Skeins of soft embroidery cotton in yellow, pink, mauve, turquoise, lime, pink, blue-green, moss green; $\frac{1}{4}$yd. narrow elastic. Adhesive; scissors; pins; large needle; tracing paper; felt tip pen; ruler.

CROSS STITCH
Bring needle out at 1 and put it in at 2. Bring it out at 3. Put needle in at 4 and bring it out again at 3. Repeat for other stitches.

DOUBLE CROSS STITCH
Make a large cross stitch. Bring needle out at centre left and put back in centre right. Out at centre top, in at centre bottom. Repeat.

1 Trace shapes and cut out. Pin to felt and cut two blue and two green fronts. Cut two pink moccasin shapes on folded felt.

2 Using tailor's chalk, rule lines on green felt shapes to match rows on pattern opposite. Embroider with cross stitch etc, as shown.

3 Embroider a row of cross stitches along straight sides of pink slippers. Run a gathering thread of running stitch round front.

4 Overlap centre back edges of moccasins. Pin and tack together. Remove pins and backstitch. Turn edge of lower heel on to heel back. Pin. Tack. Remove pins. Backstitch.

5 Embroider cross stitch patterns on the backs of the slippers, as shown above.

6 Stuff sock with crumpled paper, and fit inside moccasin. Draw gathering thread to fit sock front. Oversew slipper to sock.

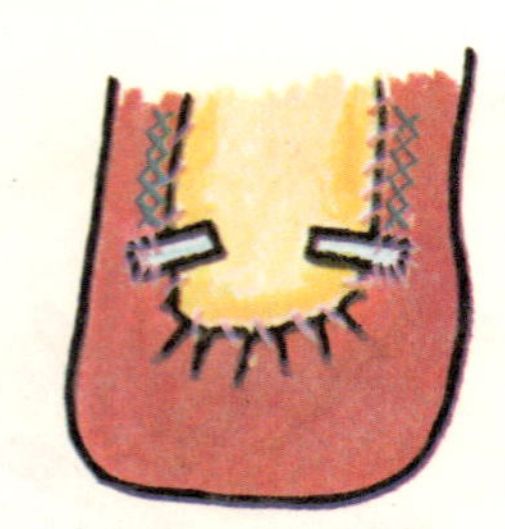

7 Cut two 1in. strips of elastic and oversew to sides of moccasin above gathered edge. Repeat 6 and 7 for second slipper.

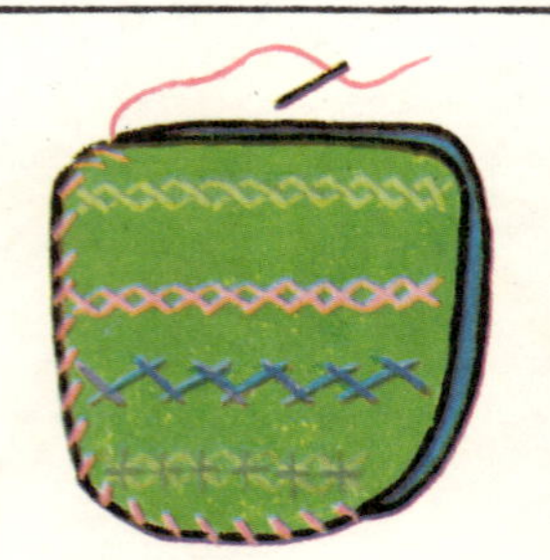

8 Place embroidered green on blue felt moccasin front. Pin and tack together. Remove pins. Oversew round edge. Repeat for 2nd front.

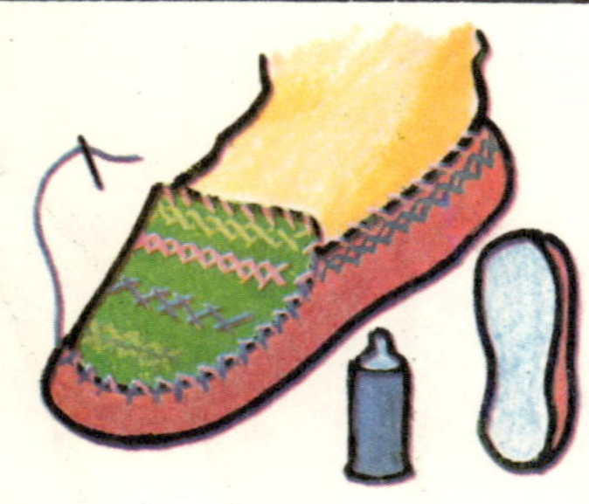

9 Pin fronts to moccasins, leaving $1\frac{1}{2}$in. open at each side. Tack. Remove pins. Oversew fronts to slippers. Glue soles in position.

MAKE A TASSEL
10 Wind coloured threads round 1in. × 2in. card. Sew across top. Snip thread at bottom. Wind thread round tassel. Stitch ends.

11 Sew long thread of tassel for lace through moccasin front. Stitch to elastic. Repeat for other laces. Make laces 6in. long.

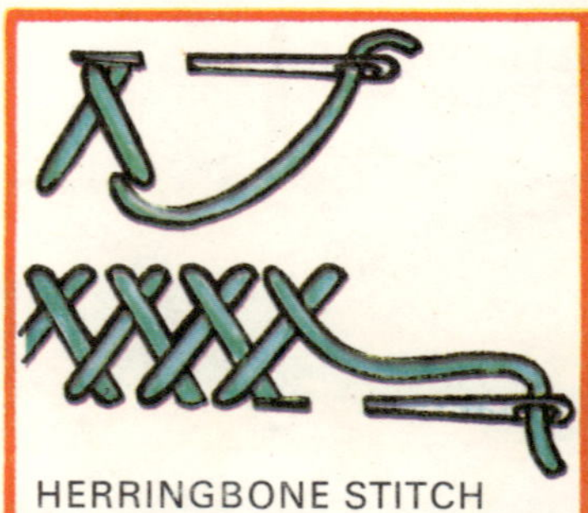

HERRINGBONE STITCH
Bring thread out below. Put needle in above right, and out left. Take thread down right, put needle in, and out, left. Repeat.

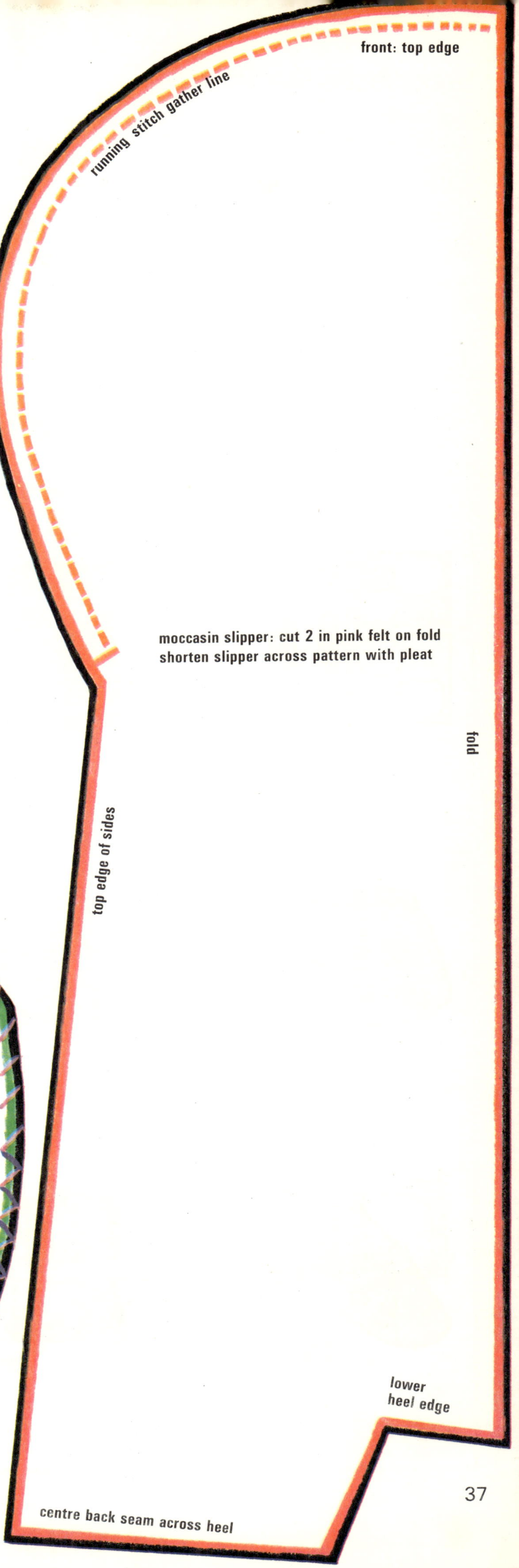

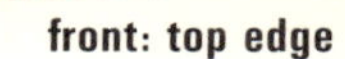

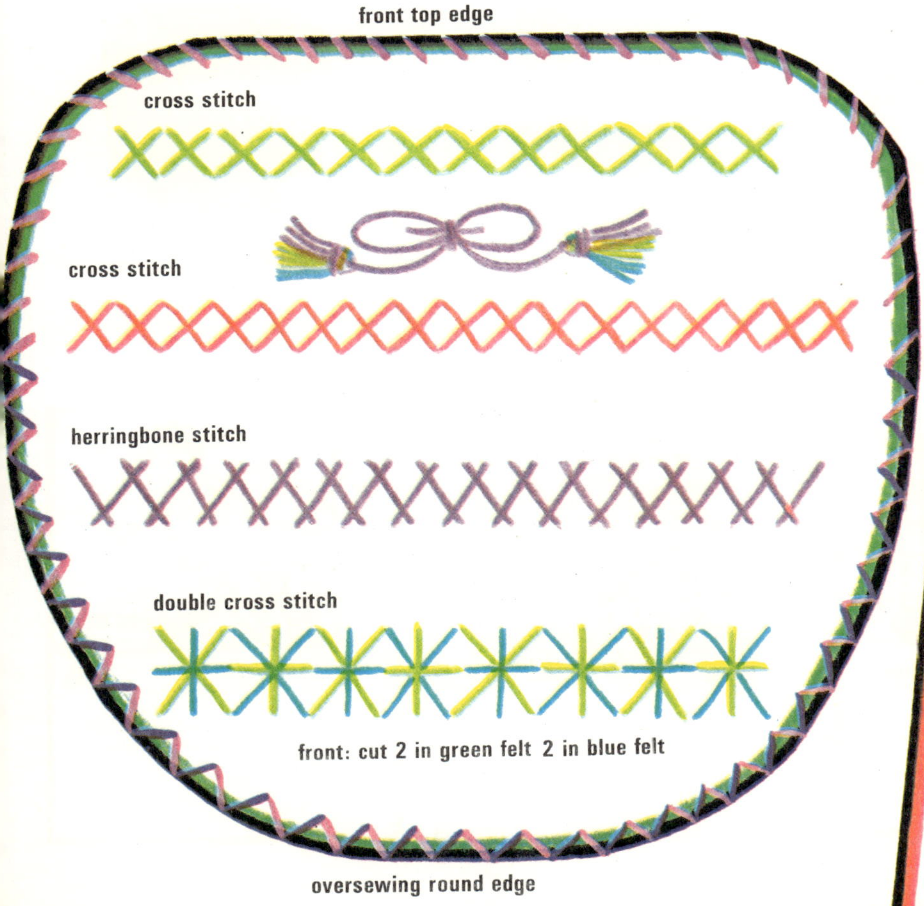

front: top edge

running stitch gather line

moccasin slipper: cut 2 in pink felt on fold
shorten slipper across pattern with pleat

fold

top edge of sides

lower heel edge

centre back seam across heel

front top edge

cross stitch

cross stitch

herringbone stitch

double cross stitch

front: cut 2 in green felt 2 in blue felt

oversewing round edge

Sun Wall Decoration

Even when it is raining outside, you can have the smiling sun cheering up your room with this bright orange and yellow felt wall decoration. It is sewn on with chain stitch embroidery and glued to a card backing. The sun is slightly padded. Other materials can be used, but allow extra to turn in raw edges.

You will need: 9in. squares of brightly coloured felt in strong yellow, light orange and dark orange; two skeins of yellow, one of blue soft embroidery cotton; a small amount of kapok or cotton wool for padding under the sun's disc; scissors; pins; large needle; tracing paper; felt tip pen; ruler. Card picture backing in same size as background square of felt: $8\frac{1}{4}$in. × $8\frac{1}{4}$in. Adhesive.

The sun shape would make a splendid cushion cover too, for small or jumbo size cushions. The shapes are easy to copy in different sizes. Cut out the background shape first to the cushion size, allowing extra for seams, and a second shape for the reverse side of the cover. Instructions for making a cushion are on pages 40–41.

For the sun's zig zag flames draw first the inner circle, then the outer circle to fit the background. Draw the zig zags between them. It doesn't matter if they are not regular. Flames never are, anyway.

The sun can be enlarged to make a poster size wall hanging too, or decorate a bedcover. Instead of chain stitch, you could use rows of buttons, or lace or binding for outlines. You could use other materials. Check gingham, printed cotton. Allow for turnings on raw edges on woven and knitted fabric. Lots of picture shapes sewn on $2\frac{1}{2}$yd. unbleached calico or cheesecloth – flowers, trees, houses, moon, stars, the sun, or just shapes – make an amusing bedcover. Why not make one with your friends?

1 Draw outlines and cut out paper patterns separately, (inner circle is $6\frac{1}{2}$in. diameter). Pin to felt. Cut out one sun and one sun face. Cut out a square of yellow felt $8\frac{1}{4}$in. × $8\frac{1}{4}$in. for background.

2 Place sun on yellow felt square, and the circle for the sun face on top. Place a small amount of padding under the circle. Tack all three layers together.

3 Sew circle to sun with chain stitch round inside edge. Chain stitch face on to circle, copying design and stitches from picture.

4 Chain stitch round edge of felt background square in blue embroidery thread. Sew long stitches in the corners for sun rays, in orange.

Room for Ideas

In this section of My Fun to Sew book, you can enjoy making all sorts of fun things for your own room. There is the bright sun wall decoration on the opposite page, and on the other pages, the pretty red ruffled lampshade, the giant ladybird floor cushions (and ideas for other cushions) and the useful odds and ends tidy. And, of all things, spider and fly insect mobiles! There is even a rag rug to make step by step. Soon your own ideas will be sparkling for other things to make.

5 Cut out a square of card 8¼in. × 8¼in. Sew a stitch through top for a loop. Knot stitch ends together. Glue picture on card.

CHAIN STITCH

1 Draw thread out. Put needle in beside point where thread came through. Bring needle out a stitch below with thread looped under.

2 Draw the thread through, evenly, and not pulling the stitch too tightly, so as to drag the material.

3 Put needle in again beside point where thread came through material, but inside loop. Repeat 1, 2, 3.

Giant Ladybird Floor Cushion

Having friends in? Listening to music? It is good to have lots of floor cushions in your room for extra seats at these sociable times.

This ladybird cushion gives you a design for one floor cushion. By following the same method you could make others even larger, plain square cushions, or made out of circles a yard across, and seamed together all round and stuffed.

Small cushions are made in exactly the same way . . . owl cushions, flower cushions. Make lots. Cushions are some of the gayest and most amusing things you can make, and help add lots of colour and design to your own room's furnishing. If you have some spare material and you don't know what to use it for, it would probably make a good cushion. Cushions can be in the shape of a big dog with floppy ears and a friendly face you can sit on and cuddle, or they can be in the shape of candy, pink and white fun fur liquorice allsorts. Cushions have been made in the shape of telephones, red lips with sets of teeth are among the many other absurd designs. Patchwork or embroidered cushions are very attractive. Just follow the methods here.

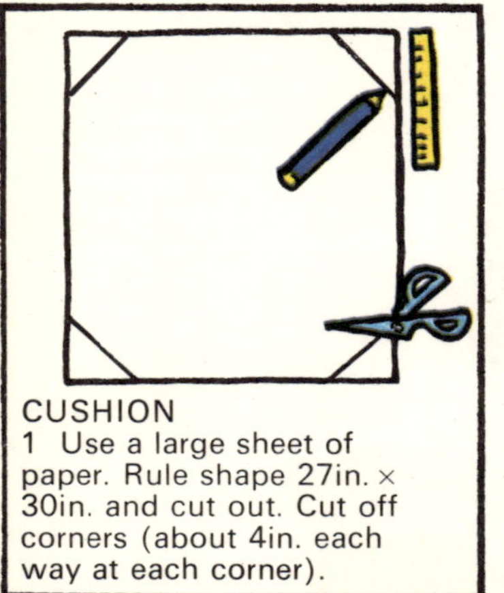

CUSHION
1 Use a large sheet of paper. Rule shape 27in. × 30in. and cut out. Cut off corners (about 4in. each way at each corner).

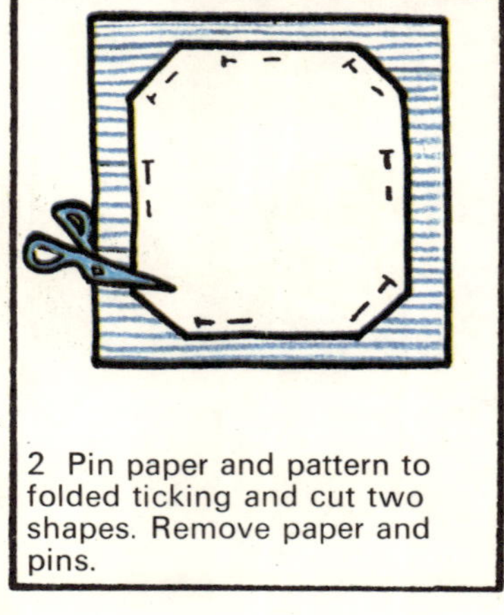

2 Pin paper and pattern to folded ticking and cut two shapes. Remove paper and pins.

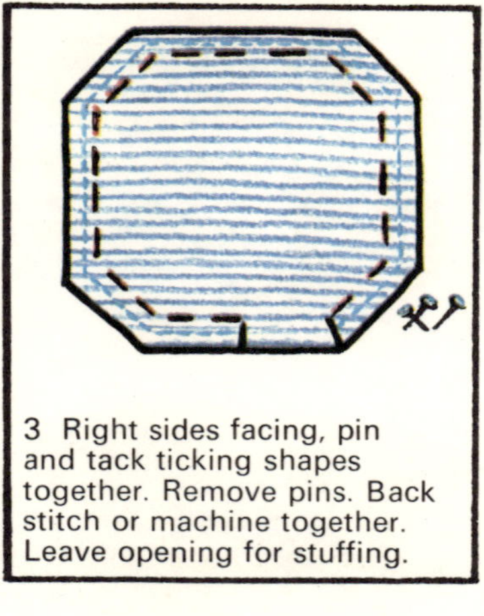

3 Right sides facing, pin and tack ticking shapes together. Remove pins. Back stitch or machine together. Leave opening for stuffing.

4 Turn cushion right side out and stuff fairly firmly. Oversew opening very securely to close and keep in stuffing.

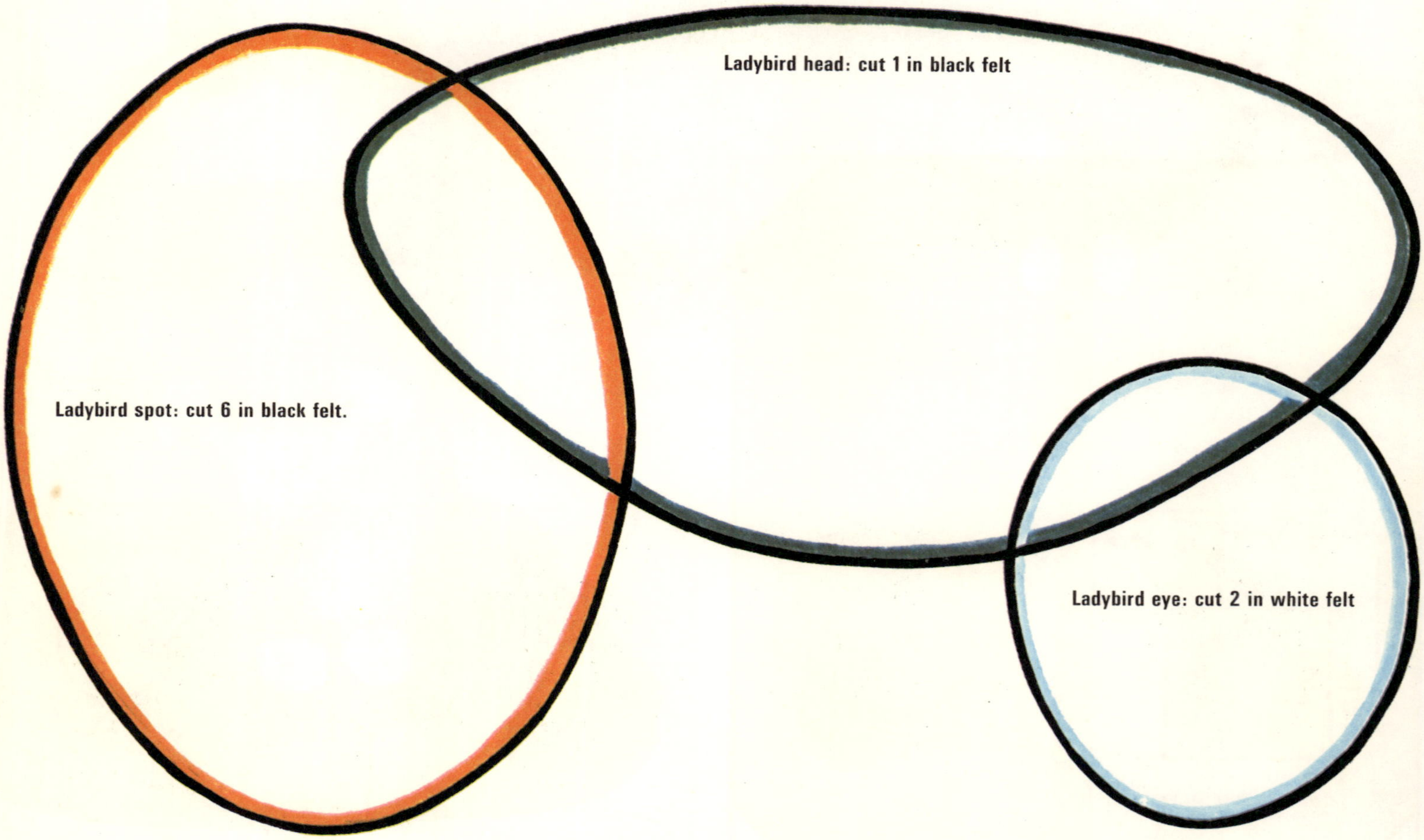

Ladybird head: cut 1 in black felt

Ladybird spot: cut 6 in black felt.

Ladybird eye: cut 2 in white felt

LADYBIRD COVER

1 Use cushion pattern. Pin pattern to corduroy and cut out one shape. Repeat with blue material. Remove paper patterns and pins.

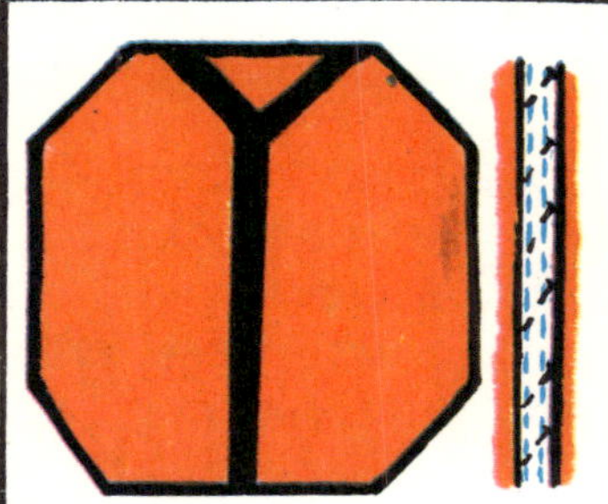

2 Mark centre of red shape with ruled line. Pin braid along it. Tack, remove pins and machine braid at edges. Sew braid diagonally for head.

3 Trace patterns and cut out one head, two eyes, and six spots. Pin all shapes in place. Tack. Remove pins. Machine, backstitch or glue.

4 Right sides facing, place red shape on blue shape. Pin and tack together, leaving end open. Remove pins. Machine or sew. Hem opening.

5 Turn cushion cover right side out. Press. Sew press studs along inside hem. Pull cover over ticking cushion. Clip press studs.

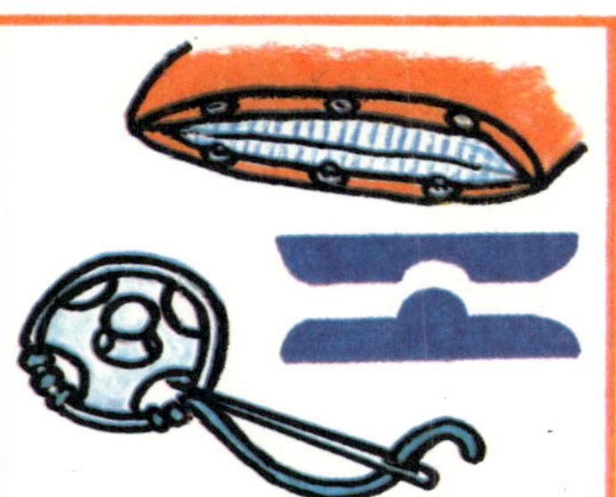

PRESS STUDS

Using a small needle sew underside stud first. Sew two or three stitches through each hole. Finish off with backstitches.

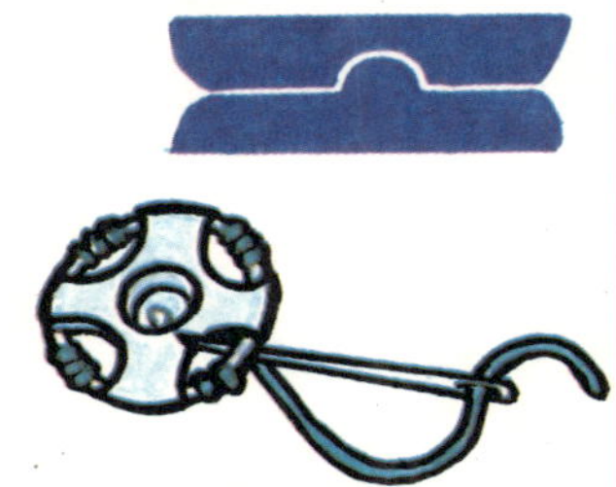

The upper side of the press stud needs to be exactly above the underside, so they fit together. Sew upper side on the same way as underside.

To save time and work instead of press studs you can sew on special tape to close the cushion opening. This tape is sold in furnishing or drapery shops or store departments. One sort is tape with press studs fastening along its length; another sort is linked by strong hooks and eyes. Velcro, a patent fastening, has a furry surface which closes when pressed together, and opens when pulled apart very easily.

You will need: Cushion $1\frac{1}{2}$ yards 36in.-wide striped cotton ticking, calico or other similar material; enough stuffing to fill cushion firmly (use kapok, foam plastic chips, cut up clean rags or polystyrene beads); Strong cotton thread. *Cover* 1yd. 36in.-wide red corduroy; 1yd. 36in.-wide dark blue hessian or linen; $1\frac{1}{2}$yds. black braid 1in. wide; $\frac{1}{8}$yd. black felt 36in. wide for ladybird spots and head; two pieces white felt 3in. × $2\frac{1}{2}$in. for eyes; white, red and black thread; five large press studs (optional); adhesive; scissors; needle; pins; tape measure; thimble; tracing paper; felt tip pen; ruler.

If a sewing machine is available, you will find it a great help when making this cushion. Use straight and zig zag stitch.

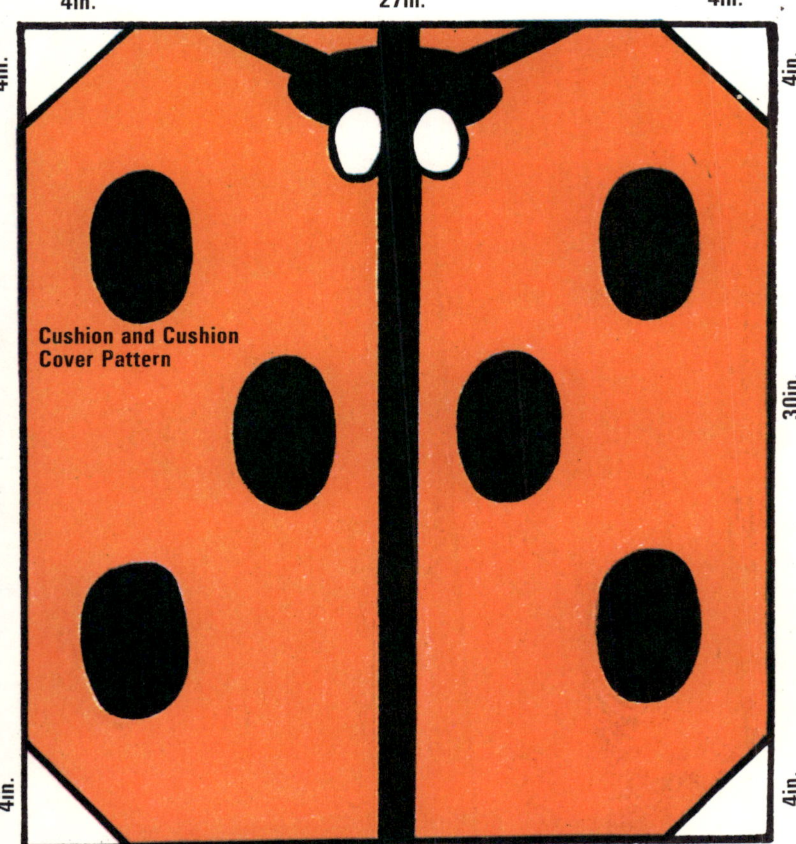

Enlarge to given measurements and cut corners from paper pattern as indicated on this chart.

Odds and Ends Tidy

This colourful odds and ends tidy, with its various pockets and fittings, is an amusing way of tidying some of the little things that so easily clutter the smartest room. It is also a useful way of always knowing where to find often needed items like scissors and comb.

There is a pocket for pencil sharpeners and paper clips; a clever needle and pincushion; the beauty pocket with false eyelashes; a special strip to pin your brooches and badges; and much more.

So often you see things in shops you would love to own, but your pocket money won't stretch to them. Those lovely plastic wall fittings with elegantly assorted moulded pockets are a prime example!

Why rely on buying something anyway, when you can make your own? By using bright coloured modern looking pieces of material, and contemporary shapes, you can give your room an ultra-modern 'wall tidy' too.

There is no need to follow the shapes in this odds and ends tidy either. Perhaps you would like a different size for your room or special pockets for your own hobby things.

The tidy is made of gaily striped deckchair canvas. It can be stiffened by narrow wood dowels being passed through top and bottom hems, and hung up. Or it can be fixed to a hardboard pin-up board.

You will need: backing: striped deckchair canvas $17\frac{1}{2}$in. × 30in. Allow for side hems if you use material without woven edges. Make 1in. hem top and bottom. Machine.

Gingham Tissues Pocket: You will need: $12\frac{1}{2}$in. × $8\frac{1}{4}$in. mauve and white gingham; 40in. crochet lace $\frac{3}{4}$in. wide. *To make:* Make narrow hems round edges. Sew lace on hems.

Beauty Pocket: You will need: 6in. × $5\frac{1}{2}$in. blue poplin; $\frac{3}{4}$yd. bias binding; false eyelashes. *To make:* Cut out shape. Fold in half from side to side, and cut lower corner in curve. Edge with bias binding. Stick on lashes.

Badges and Brooches Holder: You will need: yellow felt 7in. × 3in. Cut out with pinking shears.

Odds and Ends Pocket: You will need: black and white check gingham 10in. × $6\frac{1}{4}$in. $6\frac{1}{2}$in. piece elastic $\frac{1}{2}$in. wide. 6in. of $1\frac{1}{2}$in.-wide fringe. *To make:* Fold in half lengthways and turn in raw edges of gingham. Pin, tack and machine down sides and across lower edge. Stitch elastic across, at sides and in two places for scissors, nail file, etc. Machine fringe across lower edge.

Needle and Pincushion: You will need: 2 pieces peacock blue felt $2\frac{3}{4}$in. × $4\frac{1}{2}$in.; orange felt $2\frac{3}{4}$in. × $2\frac{3}{4}$in. Cut out with pinking shears. *To make:* Machine round two longer strips except top edge. Stuff and machine across. Machine short strip for pins on top across top edge.

Grey denim pocket: You will need: $6\frac{1}{2}$in. × $7\frac{1}{2}$in. denim; $\frac{1}{2}$yd. yellow ric-rac braid. *To make:* Hem edges; machine ric-rac braid along top, bottom and down left side. Machine a row of stitching 1in. from left.

Exercise Book and Ruler Pocket: You will need: red cotton canvas 13in. × 9in.; 1yd. white ric-rac braid. *To make:* Make narrow hems round edges and machine on ric-rac braid. Machine a row of stitching 2in. from right.

Pin pockets and felt items in correct position on striped canvas. Tack. Remove pins. Machine pockets down sides and across lower edges. Machine felt items across top.

Broken lines are stitch lines. Use backstitch or machine straight stitching

Spider and Fly Insect Mobiles

You will need: fly three safety pins; a pipe-cleaner; black embroidery thread; black ink or paint. *Lucky money spider* a pipe-cleaner; red embroidery thread; red ink or paint; scissors; a large needle.

FLY
1 Wind embroidery thread neatly along safety pin, so only top of pin shows. Sew off thread at other end.

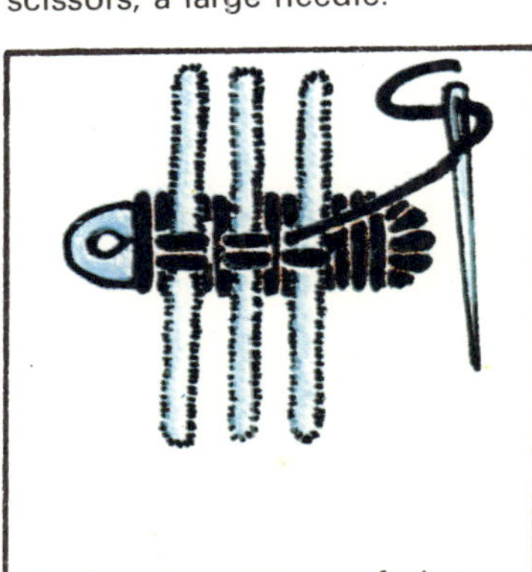

2 Cut three pieces of pipe cleaner, each $1\frac{3}{4}$in. long. Backstitch under fly for legs.

3 Place two safety pin wings on one another, and sew to fly. Ink legs and hang fly by a long string.

LUCKY MONEY SPIDER
4 Cut four pieces pipe cleaner each $1\frac{1}{2}$in. long. Cross them and wind embroidery thread round. Ink legs. Hang by a long thread.

Flowered Lawn Lampshade

A pretty flowered lawn 'granny' lampshade like this can be fitted over a ceiling light or on a lamp base, and it looks so attractive. This version has a frill round it made from the lampshade material, hemmed with shell edging (a charming way of edging you can use on clothes, too). You could give the lampshade a crochet lace frill or ungathered silk fringe edge.

If you have any of the material left over, you could glue it on a tin for a waste basket.

You will need: a curved wire lampshade frame 10in. diameter at lower edge; ½yd. 36in.-wide material; we used printed flowered lawn, but other printed lawn or cotton would be suitable. 1½yd. ¼–½in.-wide tape; thread to match material; scissors; pins; needle; tape measure; safety pin or bodkin for threading tape through hems; thimble; tracing paper; felt tip pen; ruler; sewing machine.

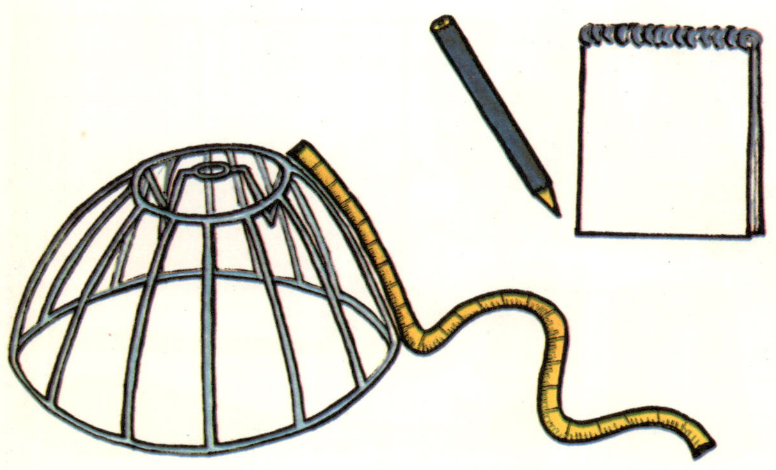

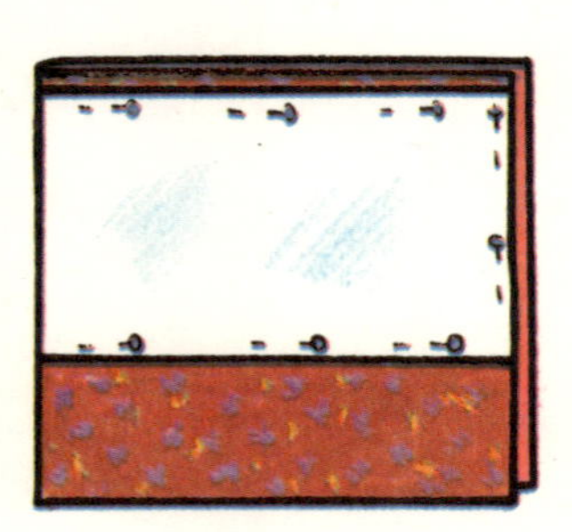

1 For paper pattern cut paper 18in. wide by depth of lampshade plus 2½in. Cut material on fold.

2 Fold material in half from side to side, right sides facing. Pin and tack. Remove pins. Backstitch or machine seams.

3 Turn ½in. wide hems top and bottom. Hem or machine, leaving an opening in each hem for threading through tape.

4 Slip end of tape through bodkin or pin a safety pin to it. Thread tape through top, then bottom hems. Leave ends to tie.

5 Turn lampshade cover right side out. Draw tapes to gather and slip shade over frame. Pin material to wire sides of frame.

6 Draw up tape in top hem to 1in. over top of frame. Draw up lower hem tape to 1in. over lower rim. Tie tape ends. Remove pins.

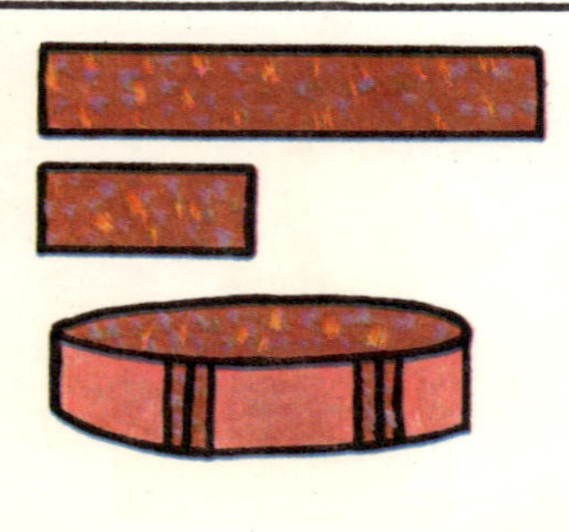

7 Frill: Cut a strip 36in. × 4in. and a second strip 12in. × 4in. Join at ends, right sides facing.

8 Turn a narrow hem at the top edge. Make a shell edge hem at the lower edge (see box No. 10). Run a gathering thread round under top hem.

9 Gather frill to fit round lower edge of shade and pin in position above hem. Tack. Remove pins, and hem top frill to lampshade all round.

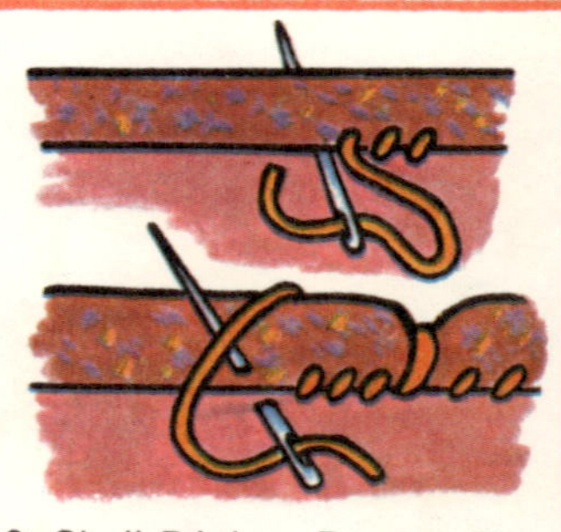

10 Shell Edging: Prepare ¼in. hem. Hem three stitches. Take thread through to right side, and over edge. Put needle in. Draw stitch tight. Repeat.

Rag Rug

Rugs made of cut wool hooked through canvas are familiar to most of us, and enjoyable to make. But if you haven't a rug kit to use, you can invent your own, for next to nothing, by making yours a rag rug. All you need is some inexpensive rug canvas, a hook, and some old clean winter rugs and coats that have been put in the jumble sale pile.

Other rag rugs can be woven with strips of wool cloth pushed in and out of loosely woven mesh. If the colour of the material chosen varies, so does the surface of the rug, and a gentle banded, uneven effect is gained. If the thickness varies, it adds to the style. This sort of rug can have a fringe or tassels knotted into the ends. It is a good idea to begin with a small rug, like ours, for practice.

You will need: 16in. × 18in. rug canvas with $\frac{1}{4}$in. holes (buy 18in.-wide rug canvas and trim); 17in. × 20in. hessian for backing rug; a rug hook or strong, large crochet hook; a straight carpet needle; extra strong linen carpet thread; scissors; pins; a large needle for tacking stitches; a thimble.
For the carpet: three different colours of clean woollen or wool weight clothes and rags. For our pyjama striped rug, we used an old black and white herringbone tweed coat given by Granny; a tartan rug that was almost new and smart red and green before a certain naughty Dalmation puppy chewed large holes in it! And a length of yellow wool left over from dressmaking.

There are sure to be several suitable items you could have to use for making your rag rug, but do be sure to check before you cut up any 'rags'. You never know—what looks like a worn out old rag to you might be somebody's favourite jacket!

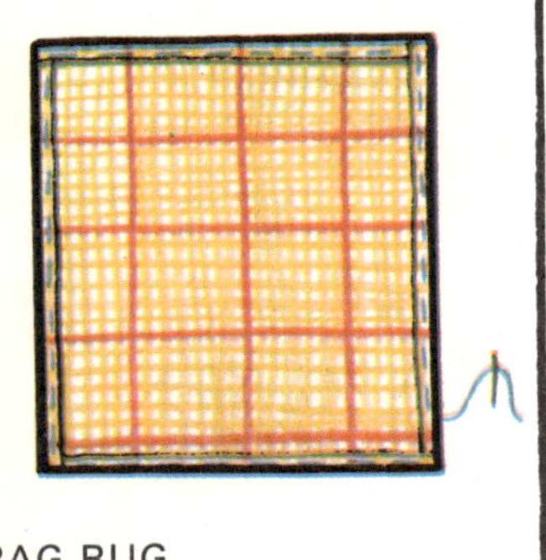

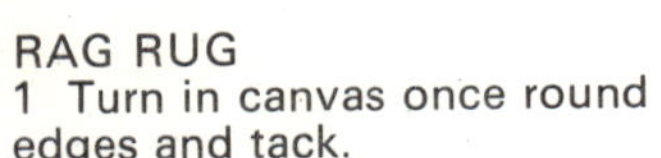

RAG RUG
1 Turn in canvas once round edges and tack.

2 From clean old rags you have been given, cut several 24in. × $\frac{1}{2}$in. strips.

3 Place strip under canvas and poke hook through to pick it up. Hook the strip through to form $\frac{1}{2}$in. loop.

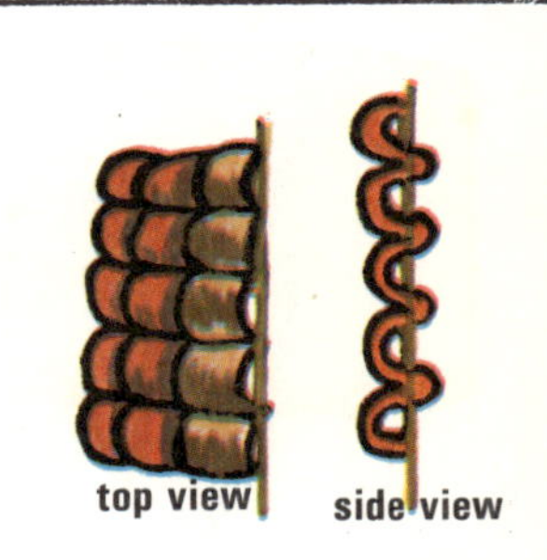

4 Work from top left. Form rows of $\frac{1}{2}$in. loops side by side. Strips should lie flat on the rug underside.

5 When canvas is covered by loops, trim the ends of the strips round the edges of the rug.

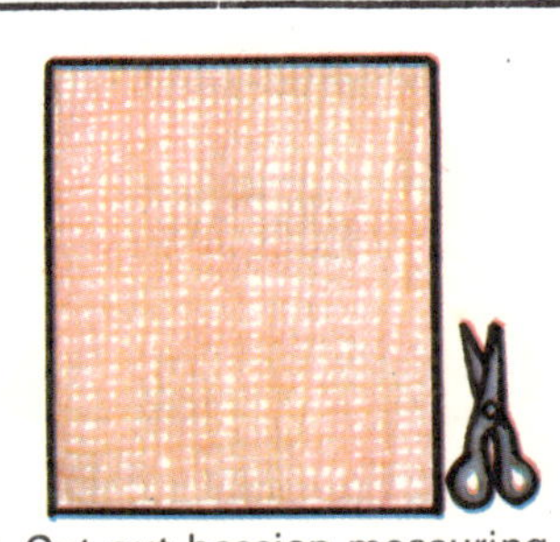

6 Cut out hessian measuring 17in. × 20in. Turn in raw edges to neaten. Make the hessian shape the same size as the rug. Tack edges.

7 Pin and tack wrong side of hessian to back of rug. Oversew together all round. using carpet needle, strong thread and thimble.

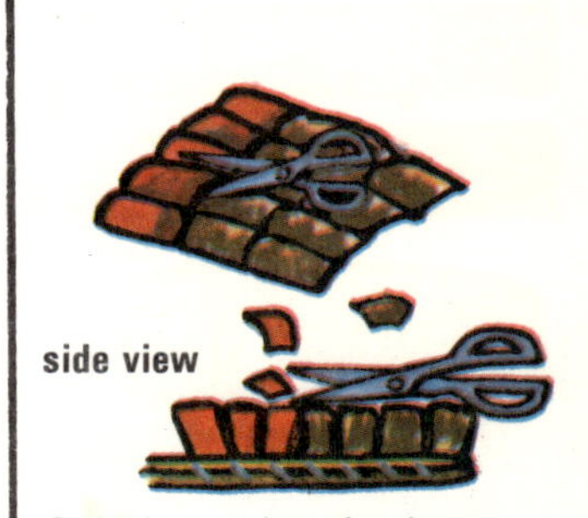

8 Using pointed scissors, carefully cut through each loop. Trim rough untidy pieces to make rug level.